Connecting and Combining

in Sentence and Paragraph Writing

Helen Mills
American River College

SCOTT, FORESMAN AND COMPANY

Glenview, Illinois
Dallas, Tex.   Oakland, N.J.   Palo Alto, Cal.   Tucker, Ga.   London, England

Special thanks to

my family—LeRoy, Marilyn, and David

the students and tutors who offered suggestions

William Strong
William E. Smith
Marilyn S. Sternglass
C. Jeriel Howard
James W. Peck
Vincent D. Puma
Muriel Harris
William McCrory
Shirley New
Nora Nishimoto

Michael Anderson
Linda Peterson

Very special thanks to

Marilyn Mills, my daughter, who wrote many of the exercises and offered suggestions throughout the writing of the book

YA
808.042
M657c
Study Skills
Writing

An Instructor's Manual is available. It may be obtained through a local Scott, Foresman representative or by writing to Skills Editor, College Division, Scott, Foresman and Company, 1900 E. Lake Avenue, Glenview, Illinois 60025.

Library of Congress Cataloging in Publication Data

Mills, Helen, 1923–
    Connecting and combining in sentence and paragraph writing.

    Includes index.
    1. English language—Rhetoric. 2. English language—Grammar—1950–
3. English language—Sentences. 4. English language—Paragraphs.
I. Title.
PE1408.M5583   808'.042   81–18468
ISBN 0-673-15317-7   AACR2

1 2 3 4 5 6-VHJ-86 85 84 83 82 81

To the Instructor

Connecting and Combining has been written for those students who need a step-by-step approach to learning to write syntactically mature sentences and incorporating them into paragraphs. The text is different from other sentence combining books because it focuses on more than just combining sentences. Rather, it helps students examine the relationship of ideas in two or more sentences before the students connect or combine them. It also breaks the study of connectors and the relationships they express into short lessons followed by exercises. In one lesson, for example, students study the connectors used to show time relationships. In another lesson they learn to use connectors to show contrast, and so on. In addition, students learn techniques such as repeating terms, substituting words for other words, deleting unnecessary words, and using the meanings of words to link ideas to make their writing cohesive. These techniques prepare them for organizing ideas and developing paragraphs and essays.

Though *Connecting and Combining* appears at first to be solely a sentence combining book, it also offers instruction in paragraph writing, beginning with the first lesson in which students study not only general and specific ideas and levels of generality but also topic sentences and developing supporting details. As a result, you can use *Connecting and Combining* as the text for a paragraph writing course.

Or you may choose to use *Connecting and Combining* as a supplementary text in conventional or individualized paragraph or essay writing courses to give students practice developing syntactically mature sentences. The text may be used, for example, as a supplement to the Building Sentences unit in *Commanding Paragraphs.* It can also be substituted for Units 7, 8, 9, and 11 in *Commanding Sentences* or used together with it.

Because *Connecting and Combining* emphasizes the relationship of ideas and the meanings of connectors, it is especially helpful for students who have had little experience choosing topics for paragraphs and organizing ideas. Students are asked to work at first with just two or three sentences; gradually they are asked to add more details and relate them logically to one another to create a longer paragraph.

The text is also helpful to students learning English as a second language. Although they may have a good background in English grammar, they may have a limited vocabulary and need detailed instruction in the use of connectors.

To work comfortably with *Connecting and Combining,* students should be able to write grammatical simple sentences, and they should also have a fundamental knowledge of the relationship and function of subjects, predicates, and modifiers, the equivalent of the lessons in the first six units of *Commanding Sentences.* Without this basic background they may need preliminary or supplementary instruction in writing grammatical sentences.

Like the texts I have written in the *Commanding . . .* series, *Connecting and Combining* can also be used for the mastery approach because it consists of study units, each of which is followed by a practice test to help you and the students determine which concepts they should review or study in more detail. Within each study unit are lessons focusing on particular aspects of cohesive writing and sentence combining. After students study the explanation of a concept in a lesson, they complete an exercise to check their comprehension and ability to apply the concept. They can see the results immediately by looking at answers in the answer key. If they have completed the exercise with only one or two errors, they can go on to the next part of the lesson and the next exercise. If, however, the number of errors reveals they have not understood the concept, they can review the lesson or ask for your help. These exercises also provide check points for you to examine and gauge their understanding of the concept. In addition, the exercises can be used as the basis for class discussion about the concepts.

At the end of each lesson you will find an assignment for writing a paragraph. You may decide, however, that you prefer to have students write only one or two paragraphs while they work on a particular study unit, especially if you are using *Connecting and Combining* as a supplement to other texts in your course.

One constructive way to give students an up-to-date analysis of their progress and their strengths and weaknesses is to use the evaluation form included in the Instructor's Manual for the paragraphs students hand in to you. This form helps you to be consistent in your evaluation, it reduces the need to write extensive comments, and it is easier for students to understand than a page or two of written comments. It also helps tutors learn how to evaluate assignments.

The Unit Review at the end of each unit brings together the concepts discussed in each of the lessons and gives students the opportunity to apply the concepts to exercises and writing assignments. Since the answers for the Unit Reviews are in the Instructor's Manual, you may decide whether you want to use the scores as the grade for the unit or whether you prefer to use the review as a practice test, giving students the answer key to check their own work. After they have completed and corrected the practice Unit Review in the text, you can then administer the Unit Review that is in the Instructor's Manual.

With a simplified concrete approach to sentence connecting and combining, students develop an understanding of how they can manipulate language to suit their purpose. As they apply the concepts they have learned in exercises and their own writing, they feel free to experiment with a variety of ways to express an idea. One benefit the students do not expect but do experience is improvement in reading comprehension. Their whole world, they tell me, changes; books they had never expected to read and understand now make sense.

If you have questions or comments about *Connecting and Combining,* please write or call me at American River College, 4700 College Oak Drive, Sacramento, CA 95841.

Helen Mills

Contents

To the Student Writer

As records, audio tapes, television, videotapes, videodiscs, and other electronic equipment began appearing on the market, some people said written communication would slowly disappear. Just the opposite has happened. The electronic media demand volumes of written scripts that can be carefully refined before they are transmitted immediately or stored for future use. Because electronics has also speeded up and improved the printing process, more books and magazines are being produced now than ever before, and people are eagerly buying them and reading them.

Even more important is the impact of electronic equipment on business and personal lives. People now collect and store information with computers, not only the financial records of companies but all the correspondence that the companies handle. Instead of depending on delivery services to carry copies of letters and reports, companies transmit their written reports by connecting their computers to those of other companies in many parts of the world. In their homes growing numbers of people are using microcomputers for keeping personal records and handling financial transactions at banks, and cable television for news, entertainment, shopping, and home and personal protection.

You are very fortunate to be living in such an exciting age because you have the opportunity to become actively involved as you educate yourself to participate in this rapid communication. To become a capable writer, you need to develop several skills. First, you must learn to gather information by talking with other people and by reading. The reading may include articles and books about subjects that interest you, textbooks, and newspapers and magazines for current events. By reading regularly, you will be more aware of sources of information for a paper than if you do no reading at all. Second, you should learn to organize the information you gather and to use it to develop your paper. Third, you should practice writing to develop fluency so that you have a ready vocabulary and your ideas flow smoothly. Fourth, you should understand the meaning of the ideas and their relationship to one another so that you can tie all your ideas together to make your writing cohesive. And, last, you should be able to revise whatever you write to eliminate grammatical errors and awkward passages. You will then be able to write a paper that people can read and understand easily.

A good introduction to such writing is learning to write sentences and paragraphs suitable for college courses and business or professional reports. The paragraph is a good beginning point for this kind of writing because you can learn to write paragraphs made up of sets of sentences that are tied together into a unit by the ideas they express. The paragraph can serve as a pattern for the longer essays and reports you may be writing later in your education or career because they have similar characteristics. The paragraph, like essays and reports, requires focusing on a particular topic, organizing the information, and carefully relating ideas, using several techniques to make the writing cohesive.

When developing paragraphs, writers often let readers know in the first sentence what the paragraph is about, and they show the organizational pattern that the paragraph follows. For example, writers begin paragraphs with a topic sentence that ties the main points together with a controlling idea. Second, they discuss the main points and give supporting details to develop them. Third, they tie ideas together with transitions and connectors between and among sentences. Fourth, they repeat necessary terms. Fifth, they maintain a consistent point of view by using appropriate pronouns, by keeping verb tenses consistent, and by maintaining a tone suitable for college writing.

If you learn the techniques that develop cohesion in writing, you will also write more readable, better organized paragraphs. The lessons in this book will help you accomplish that goal. The emphasis in this text is on the techniques you can use to show the relationship of ideas within a *set* of sentences, two or more sentences that readers recognize as a unit. Sometimes this set of sentences will be a part of a paragraph. At other times the set will make up a paragraph. The lessons will help you move gradually from expressing your ideas in short, related simple sentences to longer, more complicated sentences. Each lesson is the foundation for the one that follows. The farther you progress, the more you will be able to show the relationship of ideas in several ways. This flexibility in your writing develops with practice.

This text will help you make your writing cohesive in five ways: substituting words for others, using words to refer to other words, deleting unnecessary words, joining ideas with connectors, and using the meanings of words to link ideas.

In Unit 1 you will work mainly with sentences that each express a single idea, and you will learn how to tie these sentences together by using general and specific terms, repeating necessary terms, adding modifiers to make general terms specific, and relating ideas with pronouns and verb tenses. Unit 2 explains the meaning of connectors and demonstrates ways to relate ideas to one another by using the connectors to combine two or more sentences. Unit 3 shows how to embed one sentence within another by using relative pronouns and other introductory words as connectors.

In Unit 4 you will learn to omit unnecessary words and make your writing more effective by making it compact. Unit 5 also helps you learn to omit unnecessary words; at the same time it demonstrates the flexibility of language as you learn to use certain forms of words in more than one way. In the last lesson in Unit 5, you will use many of the techniques you have learned for developing well-constructed sentences to clarify sentences that need revision.

Having learned the techniques for making your writing cohesive, you should feel confident working on any writing assignment you receive.

Relationships Within Sentences

The parts that make up an object or living being fit together and serve particular purposes. In addition, the parts are connected so that they can function as a unit. One example is an engine, made up of many related moving parts that are linked together with connectors such as joints, couplers, nuts, bolts, screws, and springs. Another example is the bony skeleton of living beings, composed of uniquely shaped bones that are connected at the joints and held together with ligaments and muscles. If a connector breaks down or a part stops working, the whole unit may function improperly or stop functioning completely.

Ideas, especially those that you express in writing, also have to be carefully related to one another so that they form a whole that holds together to function as a unit and makes sense to readers. If the connections between your ideas in sentences and paragraphs are not clear, you force your readers to make these connections and get their own meaning out of what you have written. You can make your writing cohesive and show the relationship of ideas within sentences and among sentences by using the techniques you will study in this first unit.

Lesson 1 tells you that you can write sentences with related ideas by using a general term such as *barriers* and specific terms such as *doors, curbs,* and *stairs* to discuss the kinds of barriers that people in wheelchairs face as they attempt to move from one place to another. In Lesson 2 you learn that repeating a word such as *barriers* and using equivalent terms such as *obstacles* also make your writing cohesive.

Adding modifiers to make general terms specific is a third way, which you will study in Lesson 3, to relate ideas closely to one another. For example, you can use *two* to modify the general term *problems* in a sentence about problems drivers have had with a certain make of car. In the next sentence you can use *one* to identify the first of the two problems that drivers have had, thus tying the second sentence to the first one.

You can also show close relationships within and among sentences by using pronouns, discussed in Lesson 4, to refer to nouns in preceding sentences. When the pronoun refers clearly to the preceding noun, your readers easily connect the idea in the second sentence to the one in the first sentence.

In Lesson 5, the last lesson in the first unit, you learn that using verb tenses to show time relationships makes your writing cohesive.

All of these lessons serve as a foundation for the rest of the book in which you will learn to connect and combine two or more sentences.

Lesson 1

Using General and Specific Terms to Connect Sentences

While reading newspapers, magazines, novels, essays, and reports, you probably have noticed that the writing style of each one has distinctive characteristics. Newspaper stories, for example, usually have shorter sentences and simpler vocabularies than novels or essays. Novels in turn are different from essays because novels tell stories and essays explain ideas or give the writer's opinion about a particular issue. Each kind of writing serves a particular purpose and audience and fits into one of the following categories:

1. **Expressive writing** focuses on the writer's inner feelings, as in personal letters, journals, and diaries.
2. **Literary writing** appears in novels and short stories, drama, poetry, and songs.
3. **Explanatory (referential) writing** includes expository essays, textbooks, technical reports, histories, research papers, and so on.
4. **Persuasive writing** covers argumentative essays, editorials, sermons, and advertising.

Regardless of the type of writing you want or are asked to do, you must understand your topic thoroughly and tie the ideas together carefully in well-constructed sentences and paragraphs so that your readers understand what you have written. One method of tying your ideas together is to identify the topic in one sentence and then add specific details about it in other sentences. These sentences may be a set, two or more sentences that readers recognize as a unit, a part of a paragraph, an entire paragraph, or an essay. The number of sentences you write about a topic depends on how broad the topic is and how much detailed information you have about the topic. The amount of specific detail you need depends on how much detail you must give to make your point clear to your readers.

JOTTING IDEAS

The first step is choosing a suitable topic. You might, for example, choose to write about a general topic such as a new apartment you are planning to decorate because you want to relate something from your personal experience to your readers. Instead of keeping all your ideas in your head, you should write them down where you can see them and think about them further. By writing them down, you know that you cannot forget them, and you clear your mind for thinking about other aspects of your topic. Your list might look like the following one:

General topic:
    My new apartment on 53rd Street

Specific ideas:
    Choosing paints for the apartment
    Moving into the apartment on Saturday
    Furniture—buy one or two upholstered chairs
    Adding finishing touches to the living-dining area
    Lamp table from Bud
    Plants from Jenny and Ruth

Your list might fill a page or more as you put down your thoughts. As you look over the list, you can see that all the ideas are about your apartment and all except the second one are about decorating it. By limiting the specific ideas to a single general topic you will be able to write a cohesive paragraph suitable for a friendly letter or a personal account of your experiences:

> The apartment on 53rd Street is a big improvement over my last place, but it needed new paint in all three rooms. I decided that pastel latex paints on sale at Merv's Hardware offered the most economical way to cover the walls. Since the living-dining area is larger than the living room in my last apartment, I need at least one, maybe two, upholstered chairs. The lamp table Bud gave me and the plants from Jenny and Ruth help fill up the space. In another week or two the apartment should be comfortable.

EXERCISE 1A

Use a topic that your instructor assigns, or select a topic that interests you and that you know something about in some detail. Write about a personal experience or a job-related experience that might help readers profit from what you discovered. After you have chosen your topic, jot notes about it—at least ten—and show the list to your instructor or tutor. Save this exercise for a later assignment.

GENERAL AND SPECIFIC TERMS

To make your paragraph about decorating your new apartment more informative for your readers who may want to learn about specific ways to decorate their homes, you should narrow your focus to one aspect of interior decorating and add more details. For example, you might write about ways to make secondhand furniture look as if it all belongs together by choosing paint to create a harmonious color scheme. Or you might like to suggest places for people on a limited budget to buy furniture. The number of topics possible is very great. To explore other possibilities for a narrowed focus, you might first list general and specific terms about interior decoration:

GENERAL TERM	SPECIFIC TERM
Interior decoration	Interior architecture, finishing, furnishings

The word *furnishings,* in turn, can be a general term in relation to words that name specific kinds of furnishings:

GENERAL TERM	SPECIFIC TERM
Furnishings	Furniture, wall coverings, floor coverings, accessories

You can make each of the specific terms on the right above general in relation to other specific terms:

GENERAL TERM	SPECIFIC TERM
Furniture	Chairs, tables, sofas, beds, dressers, chests
Wall coverings	Wallpaper, draperies, murals, paintings
Floor coverings	Carpeting, rugs, vinyl, hardwood
Accessories	Lamps, vases, house plants, statues, dishes

EXERCISE 1B

List at least three specific terms for each of the following general terms.

1. building

2. plant

3. vegetable

4. wood

5. food

Show this exercise to your instructor or tutor.

LEVELS OF GENERALITY

Another way to examine the relationship of the terms about interior decoration is to list the specific terms in outline form under the general heading *Furnishings.* A numbering system for levels of generality will help you see the relationship of the parts of the outline. The number 1 indicates the most general term. The number 2 indicates terms more specific than 1; 2 also identifies terms that are at the same level of generality:

1 Furnishings
  2 Furniture
  2 Wall coverings
  2 Floor coverings
  2 Accessories

Each of the specific terms in the list above becomes general in relation to the specific terms related to each of them. The second set of specific terms is marked 3 to show their relationship to the level 2 terms:

   1 Furnishings
      2 Furniture
         3 Chairs
         3 Tables
         3 Sofas
         3 Beds
         3 Dressers
         3 Chests
      2 Wall coverings
         3 Wallpaper
         3 Draperies
         3 Murals
         3 Paintings
      2 Floor coverings
         3 Carpeting
         3 Rugs
         3 Vinyl
         3 Hardwood
      2 Accessories
         3 Lamps
         3 Vases
         3 House plants
         3 Statues
         3 Dishes

EXERCISE 1C

Show how each of the words is related to other words in the same list by numbering each word to show the levels of generality. Begin by writing 1 before the general term. All words that support the general term should be labeled 2. Words that support the level 2 words should be labeled level 3, and so on.

a. Sports
  Baseball
  Tennis
  Golf
  Football
  Soccer
  Swimming

b. Modes of transportation
  Fuel-powered vehicles
  Automobile
  Truck
  Motorcycle
  People-powered vehicles
  Bicycle
  Tricycle
  Horse-drawn vehicles

c. Liquids
  Fuel
  Gasoline
  Alcohol
  Drinks
  Water
  Tea
  Herbal tea
  Coffee

Wagon	Decaffeinated coffee
Carriage	Alcoholic drinks
Buggy	Liquor
Chariot	Wine
	Beer

Now arrange the following words in a vertical column to show their relationship to one another, and number each word as you did in the first part of this exercise:

Georgia, United States, Chicago, Illinois, States, San Francisco, Texas, Atlanta, Dallas, Los Angeles, California, San Diego, Houston

Check your answers with the Answer Key at the end of this book.

GENERAL AND SPECIFIC TERMS IN PARAGRAPHS

In looking over the list of specific topics that you might use for writing a paragraph about decorating your apartment, consider the choices given under *Accessories. House plants* might be a likely choice, now that they are readily available in many stores besides nurseries. You can write a paragraph to help people choose suitable plants for their homes by discussing three types of plants and the decorative effects they might produce:

> House plants
>> Ferns to give a lacy, soft appearance to a room
>> Tree-like plants for a lush tropical garden effect
>> Flowering plants to complement the color scheme of a room

You can see that *house plants* is a general term that represents all the plants listed below it. *Ferns, tree-like plants,* and *flowering plants* are three specific kinds of house plants. If you write a paragraph using these four terms, it will be coherent, but it will be too general to help your readers choose specific suitable plants:

Not acceptable:

People living in apartments and townhouses can choose **house plants** to suit their furnishings and preferences. They can select **ferns,** for example, to give a lacy, soft appearance to a room. If the room is quite large, the residents might choose large **tree-like** plants for a lush tropical garden effect. Or the residents in smaller quarters might prefer small **flowering plants** to complement the color scheme of the room.

What you should add to the paragraph about choosing house plants is supporting detail—the names of suitable plants so that readers can look for specific plants such as maidenhair fern or weeping fig to produce particular effects. The outline then becomes more detailed:

1 House plants
  2 Ferns
    3 Maidenhair
    3 Asparagus
  2 Tree-like plants
    3 Weeping fig
    3 Umbrella plant
  2 Flowering plants
    3 African violets
    3 Geraniums
    3 Begonias
      4 Tuberous
      4 Fibrous

When you add the names of the plants to the paragraph, readers can use the information you have given to select suitable plants for their own homes. Begin the paragraph by using the level 1 term *house plants* in the first sentence. This opening sentence is the **topic sentence,** which summarizes the entire paragraph. When readers see *people* in the subject and *house plants* in the predicate of the topic sentence, they know immediately that the paragraph is about people and house plants. The subject tells what the paragraph is about, and the predicate limits the scope of the paragraph:

	SUBJECT	PREDICATE
Topic sentence:	People living in apartments and townhouses	can choose **house plants** to suit their furnishings and preferences.

The remaining sentences are all tied to the topic sentence by level 2 and level 3 terms that give details about suitable house plants for apartments and townhouses:

People living in apartments and townhouses can choose **house plants** to suit their furnishings and preferences. They can choose **ferns,** for example, to give a lacy, soft appearance to a room. **Maidenhair** and **asparagus ferns** are especially suitable in pots or hanging baskets. If the room is quite large, the residents might choose large **tree-like plants** for a lush tropical garden effect. Two of the most popular are the **weeping fig** and the **umbrella plant.** Or the residents might prefer small **flowering plants** to complement the color scheme in the room. They can place these plants on table and windowsills. For a window facing north or east **African violets** are most suitable. Larger flowering plants include **geraniums** and **begonias,** both the tuberous and fibrous. These three kinds of plants are representative of many more that are suitable for decorating apartments and townhouses.

EXERCISE 1D

From the list of jotted ideas that you developed for Exercise 1A, choose a general term and at least three specific terms that are related to the general term, and add supporting specific information about it. Arrange the terms according to levels of generality shown in this lesson. Show your outline to your instructor or tutor. After you have revised it, save it for the assignment at the end of this lesson.

ASSIGNMENT: General/Specific Terms

After your instructor has checked the outline you developed for Exercise 1D and you have revised it, use the outline to develop a paragraph of about eight to ten sentences like the one about house plants. Use the general term in the predicate of the first sentence. Then tie the other sentences to the topic sentence by using the specific terms related to the general term in other sentences. Label the assignment *General/Specific Terms,* and hand it in to your instructor.

Lesson 2

Using Repeated Terms and Equivalents to Connect Sentences

In Lesson 1 you learned to use general and specific terms to connect sentences in a set or a paragraph. Two more ways to connect sentences is to repeat terms and to use equivalents, words that are similar in meaning.

REPEATING NECESSARY TERMS

In writing about someone or something, you usually use a noun in the first sentence to name the subject of the paragraph or essay. In the following paragraph *food processor* names the subject. Then the term is used again in following sentences that tell ways the processor saves time:

> A **food processor** saves cooks time in preparing meals. For example, a **food processor** can mince, chop, shred, slice, and grind foods almost as fast as the cook puts them into the **processor.** A clove of garlic, a carrot, or a piece of beef leaves the **processor** in small bits ready to be put into the kettle or frying pan.

By repeating necessary terms you connect sentences in paragraphs or essays and make the meaning clear to your readers. If you tried to substitute other terms for *food processor,* your paragraph would not be as clear because the other terms do not indicate the functions of the food processor as well as the term *food processor:*

> A **food processor** saves cooks time in preparing meals. For example, the **grinder** can mince, chop, shred, slice, and grind foods almost as fast as the cook puts them into the **machine.** A clove of garlic, a carrot, or a piece of beef leaves the **appliance** in small bits ready to be put into the kettle or frying pan.

Repeating nouns is especially important in writing comparisons to keep the comparison clear and make connections among the sentences:

> Piloting a **passenger jet airplane** is easier in some ways and yet more demanding than piloting a **private single-engine plane.** Piloting the **passenger jet** may be easier because it has a crew of three people in the cockpit to handle the controls, communicate with air controllers, observe the panels of dials and gauges, and watch for other aircraft in the

vicinity whereas the **private plane** has only the pilot to handle all these operations. The **passenger jet** is a much more complicated aircraft than the **private plane.** As a result, the crew members need much more extensive training and many more years of experience than for flying a **private plane.** Maintaining communication with air control may be easier in the **passenger jet,** especially the 747 and DC 10, if the **jet** has onboard computers for this operation, but the **private plane** pilot must depend on a radio for communication. Covering long distances in the **passenger jet** is easier than in the **private plane** because the **jet** can travel two to three times as fast as the **private plane** between the same points at much higher altitudes and through more turbulent weather than the **private plane.** As a result, the actual flying time for a trip between two cities is much shorter, and perhaps less tiring, for the crew of the **passenger jet** than it is for the pilot of the **private plane.** However, when the **passenger jet** travels nonstop from one continent to another, the crew members put in a very strenuous day's work because they fly for eight to twelve hours or more through several time zones.

EXERCISE 2A

Review the set of sentences in this lesson about the food processor. Next, choose a term such as *car, condominium, resort,* or any term you can write about. Then write a set of sentences—at least four or five—in which you repeat the term. Do not write a comparison. When you study comparisons later in this text, you will have an opportunity to write a comparison then.

Show this set of sentences to your instructor or tutor.

EQUIVALENTS

Besides repeating terms to make your writing cohesive, you can use equivalents, two or more words with essentially the same meaning, in place of your original key word. Such equivalents can create variety, and they can add information about the key word.

Variety

You can create variety in sentences. For example, if you use *employees* as the key word in your first sentence, you might use *workers* or the *men and women in the department* as equivalents in the other sentences:

> **Employees** in the electronics department have increased production in the past five years. Several **workers** have discovered faster, more efficient ways to assemble a radio amplifier. The **men and women in the department** should be commended.

EXERCISE 2B

Use the first word following each number as the key word in a sentence. Then write other sentences about the key word in which you use at least two of the equivalents instead of the key word. Review the sentences in the paragraph above as an example.

1. seal   mammal   amphibian   animal

2. blue jeans   clothes   pants   denims   garment

3. duplex   dwelling   building   house

4. photograph   print   image   snapshot   likeness

Show these groups of sentences to your instructor or tutor.

Information

If you are writing about a specific person, an object, or a place, you identify him, her, or it with a proper noun—Edward Fong, a Stradivarius, or Marksburg. Though you have used a specific name, readers may not know exactly whom or what you refer to. However, if you relate the proper name to equivalent general terms, readers are more likely to recognize or learn about the person, object, or place you named. The following sentences, for example, are about Edward Fong. In the second sentence he is identified as *the new electronics engineer* and in the third sentence as the *chief engineer.* In using these identifying terms, you provide information, you add variety to the sentences, and you make your writing cohesive:

> **Edward Fong** expects to simplify several wiring procedures. **The new electronics engineer** has at least three innovative ideas to improve production. **Fong** is calling on his vast experience as the **chief engineer** for the Wellington Electronics Company in New Jersey to make Logan's electronics department operate efficiently.

If you wrote about a Stradivarius, you could identify it with equivalent terms such as a *musical instrument,* a *stringed instrument,* or a *violin made by Antonio Stradivari in the seventeenth century.* Marksburg can be identified as a *castle,* a *stronghold,* a *fortress,* or a *retreat.*

EXERCISE 2C

Listed below are words that can be specific in relation to general terms. Match each equivalent general term to a specific term by writing each general term in the blanks following the specific terms. You may find three or four general terms for each specific term.

SPECIFIC TERMS

1. terrier _____

2. Washington, D.C. _____

3. butter _____

4. Abraham Lincoln _____

5. Agatha Christie _____

GENERAL TERMS

a. city b. dog c. novelist d. woman e. dairy products f. pet g. spread h. mystery story writer i. lawyer j. capital k. animal l. father m. food n. metropolis o. statesman p. playwright q. president r. fat

EXERCISE 2D

Choose three of the specific words and their equivalents from Exercise 2C above, and use them in a set of sentences. Use the specific word in the first sentence and at least two of the equivalents in two or three more sentences.

1.

2.

3.

Show these sets of sentences to your instructor or tutor.

ASSIGNMENT: Repeated Terms and Equivalents

Write a paragraph of eight to ten sentences about someone or something. Your instructor might suggest topics, or you may name someone and use equivalent terms in place of the proper name as you write about that person and his or her roles or activities. Or write about a piece of equipment such as road or building equipment, household appliances, or any other device, and use equivalent terms in your discussion. Still another source of topics is words listed in exercises in this lesson. Repeat terms, or use equivalents to make your paragraph cohesive. Label the assignment *Repeated Terms and Equivalents,* and hand it in to your instructor.

Adding Modifiers to Make General Terms Specific

You learned in Lesson 1 that you can make a paragraph cohesive by using a general term in one sentence and specific terms related to the general term in other sentences. You also learned to repeat terms and to use equivalents to tie sentences together. In this lesson you will add modifiers to sentences to make them cohesive. One modifier is the adjective, which can make general terms specific by describing and limiting nouns or extending the meaning of nouns. The other modifier is the adverb, which changes, limits, or extends the meanings of verbs, adjectives, and other adverbs.

ADJECTIVES

Adjectives may be descriptive words: **deep** cut, **bandaged** hand. They may also be limiting words: **iron** kettle, **city** streets. Or they may be determiners or possessives: **the** group, **that** plan, **Roger's** wife, **their** concerns. In each case they tell *which one.* If they are numbers or words indicating number or amount before nouns, they are also limiting, and they tell *how many:* **thirty-five** volunteers, **several** choices.

Some limiting adjectives used with a general term combine to form a new term to represent a particular item: *kitchen table, house plant, golf club, food processor, bed lamp.*

If a word ends in the suffixes *-er* and *-est,* or if *more, most, less,* or *least* appears before it, it may be functioning as an adjective that shows comparison:

the **high** cost	the **higher** cost	the **highest** cost
a **recent** report	a **more recent** report	the **most recent** report
a **favorable** outlook	a **less favorable** outlook	the **least favorable** outlook

The company's **most recent** report shows this year's **higher** cost of manufacturing electrical appliances and presents the **least favorable** outlook for making a profit in several years.

Order of Adjectives

The four kinds of adjectives discussed in this lesson usually appear in the following order before nouns:

DETERMINER	POSSESSIVE	DESCRIPTIVE ADJECTIVE	LIMITING ADJECTIVE	NOUN
the	secretary's	red	leather	briefcase
a		disturbing	telephone	call
	their	completed	accident	report
an		excellent		opportunity
	Harrison's			mistake

You can use descriptive adjectives before possessives in some cases, but the combination can sometimes be interpreted in two ways. In the following example the writer might be indicating that the hats are old or that the ladies are old:

DESCRIPTIVE	POSSESSIVE	NOUN
old	ladies'	hats

The phrase should be rewritten in either of these ways:

old hats for ladies   hats for old ladies

The next phrase with the descriptive word modifying the possessive is clear:

a hard day's work   the worried child's despair

Limiting adjectives that tell *how many* precede descriptive adjectives and other limiting adjectives:

nine triumphant baseball players

EXERCISE 3A

Identify adjectives in the following sentences by writing Adj above each word that functions as an adjective. These words may be descriptive adjectives, limiting adjectives, determiners, and possessives. To help yourself locate adjectives ask *which one* or *how many.* If you still have problems finding all the adjectives, write N above each noun and V above each verb. The remaining words should be adjectives.

```
          Adj  Adj       Adj    N    V       Adj   N
EXAMPLE:  This aluminum pressure cooker tenderizes tough meat.
```

1. Forty-three noisy children filled the small kindergarten classroom.

2. Those large, white boxes contain a blue velvet bedspread and matching draperies.

3. The nervous travelers hid their American currency and valuable jewelry.

4. Tom's wife and his eighty-year-old parents attended the college graduation

   ceremony.

5. The San Francisco museum displayed the unknown artists' paintings.

6. This season's most popular play is an old-fashioned musical.

Making Writing Cohesive with Adjectives

When you write a set of sentences, you can tie them together, as you learned in
Lesson 2, by repeating the same term. However, you frequently need something more
than the general term to connect the sentences. The following set of sentences, without descriptive modifiers for *tiger, cubs, babies, tail,* and *paws,* is understandable, but
slightly confusing:

> The **tiger** seems to enjoy **cubs**. The **tiger** lies down and lets the **babies** climb all over
> the body and head. A **cub** pounces on the **tail** and then tries to hold the **tail** in the **paws**.
> But the **tiger** whips the **tail** back and forth teasingly.

By adding descriptive, limiting, and possessive adjectives before the nouns, you add
details about general terms like *tiger* and *cubs* so that the readers' knowledge about the
tiger and her cubs gradually increases. Each adjective that you use with the same general term gives another aspect of meaning to that general term in the set of sentences.
In the first sentence, for example, readers learn that the tiger is a Bengal tiger and that
she has had three cubs. The second sentence tells readers again that the tiger is a
mother, and they also learn that the cubs are playful. Each adjective contributes to a
clearer picture of the tiger and cubs:

> The **relaxed Bengal** tiger seems to enjoy **her three** cubs. The **mother** tiger lies down
> and lets the **playful** babies climb all over **her** body and head. **One** cub pounces on the
> **mother's** tail and then tries to hold the **thick** tail in **its small, round** paws. But the **big**
> tiger whips **her** tail back and forth teasingly.

Though adjectives clarify the meaning of a noun, you should use adjectives with care.
Simply adding a long string of adjectives before each noun you use may in some cases
be like putting too much frosting on a cake:

> *Not:* The **striped, enormous Bengal** tiger seems to enjoy **her three cute, cuddly,
> playful** cubs.

Your readers will gain a clearer understanding of your explanation when you add the
adjectives gradually.

EXERCISE 3B

Add one adjective—descriptive, limiting, or possessive—before each noun in the following sentences:

EXAMPLE: The owner polished the car.

           The **happy** owner polished **her** car.
           The **teenage** owner polished the **sports** car.
           The **new** owner polished the **secondhand** car.

1. The passengers read books and magazines.

2. The restaurant serves sandwiches, salads, soup, and drinks.

3. Dancers filled the room.

4. The typist completed letters and reports.

5. The suitcase contained suits, shirts, shoes, and pajamas.

Show these sentences to your instructor or tutor.

Punctuation with Adjectives

If two or more descriptive adjectives come before the noun and they modify it equally, the adjectives are coordinate (of equal rank); the conjunction *and* can appear between them:

        soft-spoken and **considerate** counselor
        weeping and **depressed** patient
        quiet and **comfortable** and **protective** atmosphere

You may omit *and* and use a comma instead between the adjectives:

        soft-spoken, considerate counselor
        weeping, depressed patient
        quiet, comfortable, protective atmosphere

If you cannot place *and* between the adjectives, do not separate them with a comma because they are not coordinate:

        Not: **worn** and **bicycle** tire   **broken** and **glass** bottle
        But: **worn bicycle** tire   **broken glass** bottle

Two or three adjectives placed after the noun are enclosed in commas:

> The hundred-year-old house, **sturdy, elegant,** and **inviting,** escaped damage during the war.

When two or more words function together as an adjective, they are connected by hyphens:

> The fifty-five-year-old man celebrated his birthday with a well-known, self-made millionaire.

EXERCISE 3C

Read each of the following sentences. First, find each adjective by asking *which one* or *how many* and underline it. Identify figures (e.g., 120, 225) as adjectives. Then add commas wherever they are needed between adjectives. Refer to the section on punctuation with adjectives if you need help.

Sometimes overweight people decide to lose excess pounds by cutting calories. Their new diets may consist of eye-appealing taste-tempting fruit or vegetable salads. However, the unsuspecting dieters may not be aware that some salad ingredients are high-calorie foods even in small amounts. For example, kidney or garbanzo beans and macaroni potato and bean salads contain about 120-180 calories in each half cup. Even cottage cheese contributes 120 calories in a half cup, but the calories are even higher—225 calories—in shredded cheddar or Swiss cheese. The worst offenders are the delicious mouth-watering salad dressings—from 240 to 300 calories in a three-table-spoon scoop. Dieters can choose instead filling low-calorie vegetables. The list includes lettuce, shredded cabbage, regular-size or cherry tomatoes, sliced cucumbers, cauliflower buds, sliced mushrooms, carrot slices, and green pepper strips. A lemon or buttermilk dressing can also eliminate unwanted calories.

Now rewrite the paragraph, omitting the words you have underlined, and you will see that the paragraph needs modifiers to make the contents specific and to keep the meaning clear. When you omit modifiers such as *high-calorie* before *foods* or *half* before *cup,* you change the meaning of the sentences: *high-calorie foods* becomes *foods,* and *half cup* becomes *cup.*

STEPS IN COMBINING SENTENCES

When you add adjectives to a sentence, as you did in Exercise 3B, you are in effect combining several sentences. Understanding this process of combining sentences will help you eliminate unnecessary words and rearrange parts of sentences or whole sentences to clarify a paragraph you have written. However, you cannot cross out words and place word groups in new relationships unless you carefully plan these changes and know how ideas relate to one another. This lesson will introduce you to one step in combining sentences. You will learn other steps in later lessons.

In the following example you see the base sentence followed by seven sentences about the runners:

> *Base sentence:*   The runners drank juice.
> There were five runners.
> They were tired.
> They were thirsty.
> They were marathon runners.
> The juice was cold.
> The juice was refreshing.
> The juice was from pineapples.

The first step in combining is to choose a base sentence and place X before it. Then draw a line through all the unnecessary words in the other sentences. Finally, insert the remaining words into the base sentence. They are in the order in which they should appear in the sentence. In the following example, the slash marks show where you should insert modifiers in the base sentence. The punctuation to be used after each modifier appears between slash marks at the ends of the sentences:

> *Base sentence:* X The / runners drank / juice.
> ~~There were~~ five ~~runners~~.
> ~~They were~~ tired.   */,/*
> ~~They were~~ thirsty.
> ~~They were~~ marathon ~~runners~~.
> ~~The juice was~~ cold.   */,/*
> ~~The juice was~~ refreshing.
> ~~The juice was from~~ pineapples.

> *Combined sentence:* The **five tired, thirsty marathon** runners drank **cold, refreshing pineapple** juice.

EXERCISE 3D

Read each of the following sets of sentences. The first sentence in each set is the base sentence; place X before it. Then draw a line through the unnecessary words in the remaining sentences. Finally, combine the sentences by placing modifiers before or after the words they modify, and use punctuation wherever it is needed.

EXAMPLE: X   The **/** employees gathered in the **/** cafeteria for a **/** meeting.
~~The employees were~~ concerned.
~~The cafeteria belonged to the~~ company.
~~The meeting was~~ important.

The **concerned** employees gathered in the **company's** cafeteria for an **important** meeting.

1. X   The **/** manager asked the **/** crowd to listen to him.
The manager was short.   **/ , /**
The manager was bald.
The crowd was noisy.

2.   The manager made an announcement.
The manager was nervous.
The manager was perspiring.
The announcement was brief.

3.   The company could not give the employees benefits.
The company was small.
They were medical and dental benefits.

4.   Employees demanded an explanation.
Three employees were angry.
They demanded an immediate explanation.

5.   The manager begged the employees to listen again.
The manager was red-faced.
The employees were agitated.

6.   He explained that the president had authorized a raise.
The president was the president of the company.
The raise was to be immediate.
It was a 10 percent raise.

7.   The employees quickly spread the news about the raise.
       The employees were excited.
       The employees were happy.
       The news was good.

ANOTHER MODIFIER—ADVERBS

Adverbs, like adjectives, are modifiers. Some can clarify the meaning of words they modify by showing to what degree (how) something is small or prepared: **extremely** small, **carefully** prepared. Others can make a set of sentences cohesive by showing a time (when) relationship: **today, the next morning.** Or they might show a place (where) relationship: **there, outside.**

   Adverbs modify verbs, adjectives, and other adverbs. In each case they answer the question *when, where, why,* or *how.* Adverbs added to the following sentence make the words they modify specific, or they qualify or limit the words:

> The energetic child woke and played.

> The **unbelievably** energetic child woke **early yesterday morning** and played **very hard outside all day.**

> How energetic? **unbelievably** energetic
> Woke when? **early   yesterday morning**   Played how? **hard**
> How hard? **very** hard   Played where? **outside**
> Played when? **all day**

Another way to recognize adverbs is by their form; some end in *-ly:*

> The **extremely** tired child ate dinner very **slowly.**

However, not all words ending in *-ly* are adverbs:

> *Verb:*   People **rely** on John.
> *Adj:*   Tourists visited the **holy** city.

A number of words that frequently function as adverbs do not end in *-ly:*

almost	better	here	less	not	seldom	there
already	even	how	more	now	soon	too
also	ever	instead	much	quite	still	very
back	forth	least	never	rather	then	well

If you use adverbs in comparisons, you usually use *more, most, less,* and *least* before them:

actively	more actively	most actively
deliberately	less deliberately	least deliberately

The eighty-year-old man moved **more slowly** than his ninety-year-old brother. Both ate meals **less enthusiastically** than they had in earlier years.

Some exceptions are these: *well/better/best, badly/worse/worst, far/farther/farthest, far/further/furthest:*

The automobile tires were worn **badly** on the outside edges. The tires in the front were worn **worse** than those in the rear. The right front tire was worn **worst** of all.

EXERCISE 3E

Identify adverbs in the following sentences by writing Adv above each one. Also indicate whether they tell *when, where,* or *how* by writing one of these words in parentheses after *Adv.*

Adv (how)   *Adv (when)*
EXAMPLE: The **completely** automatic sprinkler system **regularly** watered the

Adv (when)
museum grounds **every morning.**

1. Carefully trained gardeners regularly mowed the recently planted lawns once a week.

2. Once a month the gardeners went out and systematically added flowering plants.

3. Soon brightly colored flowers bloomed profusely everywhere.

4. The gardeners sprayed three badly diseased shrubs once a week.

5. Eventually the shrubs died and had to be removed.

6. Visitors enjoyed the pleasantly fragrant jasmine and other sweetly perfumed

   blossoms.

EXERCISE 3F

Add adverbs that tell *when, where, why,* or *how* to each of the following sentences. The adverbs may be single words or word groups.

EXAMPLE: Ten people explored the huge, lighted cave.

Ten people **eagerly** explored the huge, **poorly** lighted cave **one afternoon.**

1. A small, slender woman showed them the way.

2. The rocky trail was damp and slippery.

3. The people could hear high-pitched sounds.

4. A small, dark-colored bird flew by.

5. Several hundred bats covered the ceiling.

6. The people left the cave.

Show these sentences to your instructor or tutor.

PREPOSITIONAL PHRASES FUNCTIONING AS ADJECTIVES AND ADVERBS

In the preceding part of this lesson you learned to use adjectives and adverbs as modifiers to extend the meaning of other words and to relate general terms to one another cohesively. The adjectives and adverbs were mainly single words, but word groups such as *later that day* and *next month,* which show a time relationship, can function as adverbs. They show when each event happened and provide connections between sentences as in the following example:

> The sample questionnaires left John's office **late one afternoon. Early the next morning** they were in Donna's office.

Now you will learn about the prepositional phrase that functions as a modifier. The prepositional phrase may function as an adverb and modify verbs, adjectives, and adverbs. Or it may function as an adjective and modify the noun that it follows. It may also function as a transition between sentences to connect your ideas. Examples of each function appear later in this lesson.

The prepositional phrase is made up of a preposition, a word such as *in, on, under, above,* and so on, followed by a noun or a pronoun that serves as its object:

PREPOSITION	NOUN WITH MODIFIERS
of	old coins
in	a small cardboard box
at	the bottom
of	a weather-beaten trunk

The phrases can be combined into a sentence. Each of the prepositions connects the phrases to the sentence:

> The boy hid his collection of old coins in a small cardboard box at the bottom of a weather-beaten trunk.

Most of the prepositions are listed below. Notice that they are mainly single words, but a few are phrases:

aboard*	below*	in*	per
about*	beneath*	in addition to	round*
above*	beside*	in place of	since*
according to	besides*	in spite of	than
across*	between*	inside*	through*
after*	beyond*	into	throughout*
against	but	like	to
along*	by*	near*	toward
along with	concerning	next*	under*
amid	contrary to	of	underneath*
among	despite	off*	until
around*	down*	on*	up*
as	due to	opposite*	upon
at	during	out*	via
because of	except	outside*	with
before*	for	over*	within*
behind*	from	past*	without*

*These words may also be used alone as adverbs:

> The dog went **out**. A cat walked **by**. The dog was not far **behind**.

Relationships Expressed by Adverbial Prepositional Phrases

The following prepositional phrases function as adverbial modifiers in sentences; therefore, **no** commas separate them from the rest of the sentence. They express the following relationships:

Position—The prepositions *in, on, at, near, above, below,* and others can tell where someone or something is with verbs such as *be, stand,* and *live:*

> John stood **in line**. He was **at the stadium**. He lives **near the ball park**.

Movement—*Into, over, behind, below, toward, past,* and others can indicate movement from one place to another with verbs that show action:

> Teri went **into the bakery**. She walked **to the counter** and bought a birthday cake. She took the large box **to her car**.

Time—*On, since, before, by, after,* and others can indicate when something happened or will happen:

> **On Monday** Jose began his new job. **By Friday** he was bored and quit.

Cause—*Because of, on account of, from,* and others tell why something happened or is so:

> **Because of the drought** the wheat production dropped drastically. Some people profited **from the farmers' misfortune.**

Purpose—*For* may express *in order to,* or it may show intended destination:

> The prospector panned **for gold.**   (in order to find gold)
> He left **for South America.**

Manner—*With* and *like* may tell how:

> The cabinetmaker worked **with precision.** He worked **like an artist.**

Means—*By, with,* and *without* can tell how:

> The people traveled **by train.** They had arranged the trip **with a travel agent.**

Adverbial prepositional phrases beginning with *despite, in regard to, except,* and other similar expressions can function as transitions between sentences; they are usually enclosed in commas:

> Some apartment residents feared for their safety. **Despite their concern,** the management refused to hire a security guard.

Relationships Expressed by Adjective Prepositional Phrases

A prepositional phrase beginning with *of* may express possession or show a relationship between the noun or pronoun that it follows and the noun or pronoun in the prepositional phrase. The two sentences in each example below can be combined into one, using *of* as a connector:

> The wishes are often unfulfilled. Children have wishes.
> The wishes **of children** are often unfulfilled.

> Walt accidentally dropped the carton. The carton contained eggs.
> Walt accidentally dropped the carton **of eggs.**

Prepositional phrases following nouns and pronouns function as adjectives and tell *which one;* like other adjective modifiers they describe, or they extend the meaning of a noun. They may begin with *in, on, above, over, beside,* and a number of other prepositions besides *of:*

Joe rubbed the top **of his head.** A small, sharp piece **of stone** had hit his bald spot. The small nick **in the skin** bled slightly and burned.

Nouns, then, may be modified by adjectives before the noun and more adjectives or adjective prepositional phrases following the noun:

> The **alert forest** ranger **in the lookout tower** saw the **orange-red** flames **from the un-attended** campfire spread to the **dry** clumps **of grass and brush.**

Comparison of Adjective and Adverbial Prepositional Phrases

The same word group may function as an adjective in one sentence and as an adverb in another sentence:

ADJECTIVE (which one)	ADVERB (when, where, why, how)
The letter **on the table** contained good news.	Jan placed the letter **on the table.**
The lamp **over the table** gave adequate light.	Sally needed a lamp **over the table.**

In the following example some prepositional phrases make nouns specific by telling which one; other prepositional phrases function as adverbs by telling when each activity took place, and they connect sentences. Other word groups functioning as adverbs also act as sentence connectors by showing a time sequence:

> Contestants **in the baking contest** prepared their favorite dishes **from nine until noon. In the afternoon** judges **from several states** sampled the entries and named the winners. **Later that afternoon** the winners received prizes **from the contest manager. The next morning** most **of the contestants** returned **to their homes.**

EXERCISE 3G

Read each of the following sets of sentences. Place X before the base sentence. Then draw a line through the unnecessary words in the remaining sentences. Finally, combine the sentences by placing modifiers before or after the words they modify, and use punctuation wherever it is needed.

EXAMPLE: X   The / office / was ready /.
~~The office was~~ new.
~~It was a~~ real estate ~~office.~~
~~It was~~ on State Street.
~~It was ready~~ for business.

The **new real estate** office **on State Street** was ready **for business.**

1. X The / manager spoke / to the / salespeople.
       The manager was experienced.   /,/
       The manager was enthusiastic.
       She spoke encouragingly.
       There were six salespeople.
       The salespeople were eager.

2.   The telephones rang.
       There were five telephones.
       They were bright red.
       They rang almost constantly.
       They rang the whole day.

3.   Customers came into the office and sat in the chairs.
       Customers were curious.
       The office was newly decorated.
       The chairs were comfortable.
       The customers sat for an hour or more.

4.   The salespeople reviewed the sales and prospects for sales.
       It was at the end of the day.
       The salespeople were happy.
       They were successful.
       There were two sales.
       There were prospects for ten sales.

EXERCISE 3H

The following paragraph is about activities that took place during a single day. First, read all of the sentences so that you know what the paragraph is about **before** you fill in the blanks. Then connect these sentences by writing adverbs, either single words or word groups, that tell when each activity took place. The first blank has a suggested answer.

   People at the writers' conference took part in several activities. ___The first hour___

they all attended a general session to hear a book publisher give suggestions for selling to the current market. (1) _____ they divided into small

groups and discussed writing and selling stories, novels, and articles.

(2) _____ the speakers addressed the groups for about twenty

minutes and afterwards conducted a group discussion. (3) _____

everyone was ready to have lunch. (4) _____ participants again

attended small group sessions. During the concluding activity the people met for a panel

discussion to ask group speakers more questions about writing and selling manuscripts.

ASSIGNMENT: Modifiers and Connectors

Write a paragraph about an event that happened over a short period of time—a few
hours, a day, or a week. It might be about preparations for an activity or about the activity itself, an argument or a discussion over a period of time, or any other suitable
topic. Use as many adjectives as you need to make nouns specific, and connect sentences by using adverbs that indicate specific times, such as *the next hour, by morning, a day later,* and so on. Label the assignment *Modifiers and Connectors,* and hand it
in to your instructor.

Lesson 4

Using Pronouns as Connectors

Even though repeating nouns is an effective way to make writing cohesive, as you learned in Lesson 2, too much repetition can make writing seem stiff and monotonous:

> A sliding glass door is both a space saver and a danger. The sliding glass door saves space because the sliding glass door does not swing out like the conventional door when the sliding glass door is opened. Instead the sliding glass door moves out of the way on a track parallel to a glass window the same size as the sliding glass door. However, the sliding glass door can be a danger when people try to walk through the closed sliding glass door because they think the sliding glass door is open.

The technique used most frequently to tie sentences together is substituting pronouns for the repeated nouns. In the sentences above the pronoun *it* can be used several times in place of *sliding glass door* if the pronoun refers clearly to the noun:

> A sliding glass door is both a space saver and a danger. **It** saves space because **it** does not swing out like the conventional door when the sliding glass door is opened. Instead **it** moves out of the way on a track parallel to a glass window the same size as the sliding glass door. However, **it** can be a danger when people try to walk through the closed door because they think **it** is open.

Another way to tie sentences together is using appropriate pronouns to maintain a consistent point of view. Point of view indicates the way you see the subject you are writing about. In this lesson you will learn when to substitute pronouns for nouns and how to maintain a consistent point of view that shows the relationship of ideas.

PERSONAL PRONOUNS

Though most pronouns, such as *everyone, each, several, both,* and others, keep the same form wherever they are used in a sentence, one group, the personal pronouns, may have as many as four forms. The subjective forms can be used as subjects or subject complements. The objective forms can be used as objects in sentences. One form of the possessives is used with nouns and functions as an adjective. The other form of the possessives may function as either a subject or an object. The following chart shows the forms of the personal pronouns:

	SUBJECTIVE	OBJECTIVE	POSSESSIVE SUBJECTIVE OBJECTIVE	POSSESSIVE ADJECTIVE
Singular				
First person	I	me	mine	my
Second person	you	you	yours	your
Third person (M)*	he	him	his	his
(F)*	she	her	hers	her
(N)*	it	it	its	its
Plural				
First person	we	us	ours	our
Second person	you	you	yours	your
Third person	they	them	theirs	their

*Masculine, Feminine, Neuter.

When you use personal pronouns, you not only tie the sentences together, but you also discuss your topic from a particular point of view. Point of view indicates the way you see the topic you are writing about. You may tell about your personal observations and ideas by using *I*, you may address your readers by using *you*, or you may write as an observer about something by using *he, she, it,* and *they.*

The following sections give details about personal pronouns and the points of view they express.

First-Person Pronouns

I/me/my/mine (singular)
we/us/our/ours (plural)

If you discuss a subject from your personal viewpoint, use *I*, the first-person pronoun, to refer to yourself each time you say something about yourself. This is the subjective (personal or internal) point of view of the speaker or writer:

Not: I went for a physical examination; **you** get pinched with needles, and the doctor attaches **you** to all kinds of machines.

But: I went for a physical examination; I was pinched with needles, and the doctor attached **me** to all kinds of machines.

The writer should not have used *you* in the second part of the original sentence because the experience was the writer's, not the reader's. Using *I* in the second part of the sentence connects it to the first part and keeps the point of view the same in both parts.

If you write a report in which you present the opinion of yourself and others, use *we* and *us,* the first-person plural pronouns, to represent all of you:

> **We** expect cooperation if the manager expects **us** to reorganize the department effectively.

Second-Person Pronouns

> *you/your/yours* (singular and plural)

If you are giving directions to the reader, use *you,* the second-person pronoun through-out because you are addressing the reader. Second person is also the subjective point of view. You may use the pronoun *you* or the command form of the verb with *you* understood. In the following sentence *pack* is the command form of the verb; it means *you pack:*

> **You** need mainly sports clothes for the trip, but pack at least one party outfit for **your** evenings on the town.

Third-Person Pronouns

> *he/him/his* (masculine singular)
> *she/her/hers* (feminine singular)
> *it/its* (neuter singular)
> *they/them/their/theirs* (masculine, feminine, neuter plural)

If you write about someone or something, use *he, she,* and *it,* third-person singular pronouns, or *they,* the third-person plural pronoun, to replace or refer to nouns or indefinite pronouns, which are also third person. This is the objective (impersonal) point of view:

> The **man** and **his wife** rented a car in Europe. **He** drove most of the time while **she** photographed **him** and people and towns along the way. Occasionally **he** took pictures of **her. They** spent four days driving through England. **Both** thoroughly enjoyed **their** vacation.

MAINTAINING CONSISTENT POINT OF VIEW

For most college and business writing use nouns and third-person pronouns to maintain an objective (observer's or external) point of view. You cannot mix first-person or second-person pronouns as in the following example:

> *Not:*   Video cassettes make full-length motion pictures and college courses available to people who have the appropriate playback equipment. **You** can watch a motion picture without interruption by TV commercials. Or **we** can watch the same tape of a college lecture over and over until **we** understand clearly all the points the lecturer has made. Video cassettes are a worthwhile convenience.

To make point of view consistent, change the pronouns *you* and *we* to the plural third-person pronoun *they* because *they* should refer to the plural noun *people.* The paragraph, with the changes made, should look like this:

> *But:* Video cassettes make full-length motion pictures and college courses available to people who have the appropriate playback equipment. **They** can watch a motion picture without interruption by TV commercials. Or **they** can watch the same tape of a college lecture course over and over until **they** understand clearly all the points the lecturer has made. Video cassettes are a worthwhile convenience.

EXERCISE 4A

Make point of view consistent in the following passage by changing pronouns to third-person forms. Draw a line through the words to be changed, and write the revision above them.

People look forward to spring and summer and to the ripening of fruit. Many

people have fruit trees in their yards. You eat as much fresh fruit as you want, and

then you preserve the rest. They often make jams and jellies to eat in the winter. You

find cleaning the fruit the most time consuming. We then cook the fruit with sugar for

a few minutes and afterwards add a fruit pectin. Next, we store it in tightly sealed

glass jars. They enjoy opening a jar of the preserved fruit during the fall and winter.

INDEFINITE PRONOUNS

Indefinite pronouns, as their name suggests, refer to general groups of people or things rather than to specific persons or things. They are all third person. They function as subjects or objects. Some of them may function as adjectives before nouns: **each** item, **several** people. A few of them can be made possessive by adding -*'s:* **everybody's** concern. The indefinite pronouns do not refer to preceding nouns, but the third-person pronouns *he, she, it,* and *they* can refer to them. The following words may function as indefinite pronouns.

1. The following indefinite pronouns are always singular:

another	anything	everybody	much	no one	somebody
anybody	each	everyone	neither	nothing	someone
anyone	either	everything	nobody	one	something

One of my friends rented an apartment. **Everything** is wrong with it.

2. The following indefinite pronouns are always plural:

> both   few   many   several

> **Several** of the boats were damaged. John later examined **many** of them.

3. The remaining indefinite pronouns may be either singular or plural, depending on how they are used in sentences:

> all   any   enough   none   some

> **Any** of the information is valid. **Any** of the reports are available.

DEMONSTRATIVES

This/these and *that/those* may function as adjectives before nouns to show nearness to or distance from a point. These same words can be used alone as pronouns. They make writing cohesive because they refer to a preceding noun. In the following example *that* indicates the other pen:

> *Adjective:*   **This** pen has enough ink.
> *Pronoun:*   **That** needs a refill.

In the next example *these* and *those* refer to *grapes:*

> The grapes may be ready for harvesting. **These** near the house taste sweet. **Those** near the barn need a few more days on the vine.

EXERCISE 4B

Write sentences using the following words as pronouns.

1. anyone

2. something

3. both

4. all

5. one

6. this

7. those

Show these sentences to your instructor or tutor.

PRONOUN-ANTECEDENT AGREEMENT

Although repetition of key nouns (Lesson 2) is an effective way to keep the relationship of ideas clear, you do not always repeat every noun you use if you can use a pronoun that clearly refers to the noun. The third-person pronouns *he, she, it,* and *they* can refer to and replace nouns, which are also third person. To make writing cohesive, use a noun such as *climate* or *storms* to name what you are discussing. In other sentences about the same subject you can often replace each noun with a third-person pronoun that will refer to the noun: *it* can replace *climate,* and *they* can replace *storms:*

> The year-round **climate** is moderate. It changes only slightly from season to season.
> **Storms** hit the area rarely; however, **they** can be destructive.

The noun that the pronoun refers to is called the *antecedent,* which means *going before. Climate* is the antecedent of *it,* and *storms* is the antecedent of *they.* If you use the wrong form of the pronoun, your readers may have to reread the sentence to try to figure out what you mean. Your instructor might use the correction symbol *PA Agr* to indicate a pronoun-antecedent agreement problem.

Singular Antecedent—Singular Pronoun or Possessive

1. If the noun is singular, the pronoun or possessive must be singular:

> *Antecedent*   *Pronoun*
> **Dolores**   is the buyer for the paint department. **She**   enjoys working with colors.

Because the noun *Dolores* in the preceding example names a woman, you must use the feminine form of the third-person pronoun *(she)* to refer to *Dolores. Dolores* is the antecedent of the pronoun *she.*

2. Singular indefinite pronouns such as *anybody, each, everyone, neither,* and *something* are replaced by singular pronouns or possessives *(his, her, its):*

> *Antecedent*   *Possessive*   *Antecedent*
> **Everyone**   selects **his** or **her** favorite color. **Each**   of the customers reveals
>
>   *Possessive*
> something about **his** or **her** personality.

3. Collective nouns such as *group, jury, band, committee,* and *team* are replaced by singular pronouns or possessives if the group works or acts as a unit:

> The **jury** reached **its** verdict.   (Unanimous agreement)

EXERCISE 4C

Write a set of five sentences about a single topic. In the first sentence use one or more singular nouns. In the other sentences use pronouns or possessives in place of the nouns, or repeat the singular nouns. Draw arrows from the pronouns and possessives to the nouns they replace. Show these sentences to your instructor or tutor.

Plural Antecedent—Plural Pronoun or Possessive

1. If the noun is plural, the pronoun or possessive must be plural:

> *Antecedent*   *Possessive*   *Pronoun*
> The **campers**   packed **their**   car for the trip. **They**   drove the cars into the
> campsite at nightfall.

2. Two or more nouns joined by *and* are replaced by plural pronouns or possessives:

> *Antecedents*   *Possessive*   *Pronoun*
> **Michael and his sister** watch **their**   weight constantly. **They**   eat very little.

3. Plural indefinite pronouns such as *both, many,* and *several* are replaced by plural pronouns or possessives:

> **Many** of the employees like **their** jobs. **Several** are unhappy with **their** pay. **They** could be made happy with a pay increase.

4. Collective nouns such as *group, jury,* and *band* are replaced by plural nouns and possessives if the group works or acts as a number of individuals:

> The **jury** ordered **their** meals before beginning deliberation.   (Individual choice)

EXERCISE 4D

Write a set of five sentences about a single topic. In the first sentence use one or more plural nouns. In the other sentences use pronouns and possessives in place of the nouns, or repeat the plural nouns. Show these sentences to your instructor or tutor.

AVOIDING AWKWARD PRONOUN USAGE

Paragraphs that focus on people involve the readers and hold their interest better than those that focus on objects or ideas and refer to people indirectly. However, if you use a singular noun or pronoun, such as *person, student,* or *everyone,* that may refer to either a man or a woman, you will have to use singular pronouns to refer to the nouns. To acknowledge both sexes you should use *he or she, him or her,* or *his or her* to refer to the singular noun. You can avoid the awkwardness of repeating both pronouns several times by using a plural noun and referring to it with *they, them,* or *their:*

> *Acceptable:*   The **person** who travels frequently should invest in a strap to hold **his or her** suitcase closed. Then **he or she** will not have to face an open suitcase coming down the airport baggage ramp.

> *But:*   **People** who travel frequently should invest in a strap to hold **their** suitcases closed. Then **they** will not have to face an open suitcase coming down the airport baggage ramp.

One is another word that sometimes causes awkwardness. Again, using plural nouns and plural third-person pronouns eliminates the problem:

> *Awkward:*   **One** sometimes hesitates to try something new, but **one** must take some chances, especially if **one** does not put **oneself** in danger.

> *Improved:*   **People** sometimes hesitate to try something new, but **they** must take some chances, especially if **they** do not put **themselves** in danger.

FAULTY PRONOUN REFERENCE

As long as the pronouns you use refer to particular nouns or pronouns, your readers should have no problem understanding what you have written. However, if pronoun reference is unclear, your readers will feel confused, and your instructor might use the correction symbol *Ref* to indicate faulty pronoun reference. For example, the second sentence in the following example is unclear because *he* can refer to either Brian or Don. As a result, readers cannot tell whether Brian or Don is the one with problems:

> Brian and Don spend hours talking together. He needs someone to listen to his problems.

The second sentence has to be rewritten with the name of either man in place of *he:*

> Brian needs someone to listen to his problems.   *or*   Don needs someone to listen to his problems.

If you write a sentence in which you use two singular nouns or two plural nouns, you may have to repeat the nouns to avoid confusing your readers instead of using pronouns, especially if both nouns name people:

Not:	Sally called Sarah because she wanted her to write a letter of recommendation.
But:	Sally called Sarah because Sally wanted Sarah to write a letter of recommendation.
Or:	Sally called Sarah because Sarah wanted Sally to write a letter of recommendation.
Or:	In a telephone call Sally asked Sarah to write a letter of recommendation.

If you use pronouns such as *they* or *it* in the following examples without an antecedent, the meaning will not be clear:

Not:	**They** repair cars all day.
But:	The **mechanics** repair cars all day.

Not:	**It** was a victory.
But:	The **decision** was a victory.

You may find yourself beginning a sentence with *this* or *it* to refer to a preceding idea instead of to a specific noun. This kind of reference is acceptable if you use it once or twice in a paper, but if you use these pronouns without antecedents many times, the relationship of the ideas you are expressing will become fuzzy. If your readers put ideas together differently from what you had intended, they may not be able to figure out what you are trying to say. The first example can be interpreted in more than one way because *this* and *it* do not give readers a specific idea about what the writer intends to say:

> Some athletes enter competitions to break old records. **This** may put greater strain on their bodies and minds than they can endure. **It** may even mean the end of their competing in future athletic events.

The next two examples show the set of sentences above rewritten with different nouns replacing *this* and *it:*

> Some athletes enter competitions to break old records. **Such a goal** may put greater strain on their bodies and minds than they can endure. **Resulting injuries** may even mean the end of their competing in future athletic events.

> Some athletes enter competitions to break old records. **This kind of competition** may put a greater strain on their bodies and minds than they can endure. **The undue stress** may even mean the end of their competing in future athletic events.

EXERCISE 4E

Underline the pronoun or possessive in the following sentences. If it does not agree with the noun it refers to, write the acceptable form above. If pronoun usage is awkward, use nouns in place of some of the pronouns and use other pronouns.

1. Maria and Paul are expert cooks, and they create a variety of gourmet meals in

   their restaurant and at home.

2. Friends who dine with them receive the surprise of a lifetime when he brings in a plate of flaming shishkabobs.

3. Another of his specialties is preparing the after-dinner "Devil's Cup" with flaming liqueurs, coffee, and mounds of whipped cream.

4. She specializes in preparing a delicate chocolate mousse.

5. Each of the meals is served on their own special platter.

6. Maria's music group holds their monthly meetings in the restaurant.

7. After the meeting each member of the group orders their favorite meal.

8. Both take courses from time to time to learn to prepare other kinds of food.

9. They test the recipes at home before preparing it in the restaurant.

10. One can learn to be a gourmet cook if one has the time and the desire, but one usually has other interests competing for one's time.

ASSIGNMENT: Pronouns

Write a paragraph of eight to ten sentences. Your instructor may suggest a topic, or you may write about people and the things they do. Write the paragraph in the third person, using *he, she, it,* or *they* to refer to nouns. Use pronouns in place of nouns whenever the pronoun can clearly refer to the noun it replaces. Draw arrows from the pronouns to the nouns they replace. Label the assignment *Pronouns,* and hand it in to your instructor.

Lesson 5

Making Connections with Verbs

In addition to making your writing cohesive by using techniques you have learned in the first four lessons, you can maintain a consistent point of view with verb tenses that show time relationships. You also have the opportunity to make your writing lively and vigorous in two ways.

First, you can replace frequently used verbs with sharper, stronger verbs that convey your meaning precisely. For example, instead of using *follow* with adverbs such as *closely, steadily,* or *stealthily,* you can use a number of verbs that will give a more dynamic picture of the action. Each verb changes the meaning of the sentence slightly:

> The detective **followed** the suspect.
> The detective **pursued** the suspect.
> The detective **hunted** the suspect.
> The detective **trailed** the suspect.
> The detective **shadowed** the suspect.
> The detective **tracked** the suspect.
> The detective **hounded** the suspect.

In choosing verbs be sure that you understand the meaning of the word that you select. In addition, select words that fit in with your writing style. Using *interrogate* instead of *question* might sound impressive, but *question* may be more appropriate in your particular sentence than *interrogate:*

> The detective **questioned** the suspect for hours.
> The detective **interrogated** the suspect for hours.

Second, you can often change nouns ending in suffixes such as *-tion, -sion, -ance,* and *-ence* to verbs and thereby eliminate unnecessary words. Here are some examples:

> *Not:* The committee reached a decision to accept the proposal.
> *But:* The committee decided to accept the proposal.

> *Not:* The man's appearance gave the impression of his being frightened.
> *But:* The man appeared to be frightened.

EXERCISE 5A

Listed below are overworked verbs. Write three other verbs that you might use in place of the verb given to make a sentence dynamic. Then use each new word in a sentence. Use a dictionary or a book like *Roget's Thesaurus* to find words related to those listed.

EXAMPLE: move—slide, glide, roll

> The skier **moved** down the mountain.
> The skier **slid** down the mountain.
> The skier **glided** down the mountain.
> The skier **rolled** down the mountain.

1. run

2. fall

3. ask

Show these sentences to your instructor or tutor.

EXERCISE 5B

Listed below are nouns ending in *-tion, -sion,* and *-ance.* Write the verb form for each noun in the blank to the right. Then write two sentences; use the noun in the first one and the verb in the second one.

EXAMPLE: congratulations   Verb _____congratulate_____

> Linda Wells offered her congratulations to the professor on his promotion.
> Linda Wells congratulated the professor on his promotion.

1. confusion   Verb _____

2. disappearance   Verb _____

3. examination   Verb_____

Show these sentences to your instructor or tutor.

TIME RELATIONSHIPS

Although you probably use appropriate verb tenses to show time relationships when you talk about events taking place, you may not be consciously aware of each of the tenses, and, therefore, you sometimes fail to keep tenses consistent when you write. If you change tenses without reason, you may confuse your readers:

> *Not:*   The sky **darkened.** Then rain **falls.** People **will open** their umbrellas.
> *But:*   The sky **darkened.** Then rain **fell.** People **opened** their umbrellas.

If you want to show that one event happened before another one, you can use appropriate tenses of verbs to show which event happened first and which one second:

> The weather forecaster **had reported** showers. People **expected** rain.

You can also show the time events took place by adding adverbs that tell *when* something happened:

> *When (time):* People expected rain. **Earlier (The day before)** the weather forecaster had
> predicted showers. (When? Earlier or The day before)

Certain adjectives, modifiers that tell *which one* and *how many,* can also show the sequence of events:

> People expected rain. The **morning** forecast had predicted showers. (Which forecast?
> The morning forecast)

Time is divided into two parts—the past and the future—by the present:

_____ X_____
Past   Present   Future

The way to indicate the past, present, or future is to use particular verb tenses. *Tense* refers to the time something happened and how long it went on. Sometimes you can write about an event using only the past tense, or you may use the future tense in several sentences to discuss plans for the future. More frequently you will find that something you write about takes place over a period of time. Therefore, you have to use a verb tense that tells what happened in the past, another verb tense to show that one event happened before another, and a third tense to tell what will happen in the future. By using appropriate verb tenses, you will help your readers understand clearly when each event took place. Here is a summary of verb tenses:

Simple and Perfect Tenses

PAST	Past perfect	The meeting **had begun.**
	Past	The meeting **began.**
	Present perfect	The meeting **has begun.**
PRESENT	Present	The meetings **begin.** The meeting **begins.**
FUTURE	Future	The meeting **will begin.**
	Future perfect	The meeting **will have begun.**

Progressive Tenses

PAST	Past perfect	The members **had been arriving.**
	Past	The members **were arriving.**
	Present perfect	The members **have been arriving.**
PRESENT	Present	The members **are arriving.**
FUTURE	Future	The members **will be arriving.**
	Future perfect	The members **will have been arriving.**

VERB PARTS

The tenses are formed by using the five parts of the verb shown in the chart below. They are arranged in this order because you will find the parts of the verb, *prepare* and *begin,* for example, listed in this way in many dictionaries:

Part 1 (Base)	Part 2 (Verb + *s*)	Part 3 (Past)	Part 4 (V-ed)	Part 5 (V-ing)
prepare	prepares	prepared	prepared	preparing
begin	begins	began	begun	beginning

The parts are used to indicate the following tenses:

Part 1   present tense with plural nouns and pronouns and *I* and *you* future tense with auxiliary (helping) verbs

Part 2   present tense with singular nouns and pronouns

Part 3   past tense

Part 4   present perfect tense with auxiliary verbs
past perfect tense with auxiliary verbs
future perfect tense with auxiliary verbs

Part 5   all the progressive tenses with auxiliary verbs

VERB TENSES

The section that follows explains how each of the five verb parts are used to form all the verb tenses, and it explains each verb tense. Verbs for present and past tenses are single words. Verbs for other tenses are verb phrases consisting of one or more auxiliary (helping) verbs and the main verb. Negatives such as *not* and *never* are **not** a part of the verb phrase.

Present Tense

The present tense is used to discuss or write about something that is happening now. It is formed by using either Part 1 (Base) or Part 2 (Verb + *s*) of a verb, depending on whether the subject is singular or plural.

a. Part 1 (Base) of the verb, the form that appears in dictionaries, is used with plural nouns and pronouns and the pronoun *I.* The subject may be a plural noun such as *friends* or two or more nouns joined by *and:*

> The two friends **meet** for the first time in several years.
> Harriet and Leon **sit** in the lounge of the ski lodge.

The verb *be* has three forms for Part 1: *am, are,* and *be:*

> I **am** a skier. My friends **are** skiers. (You) **Be** careful.

b. Part 2 (Verb + *s*) of most verbs is formed by adding *-s* or *-es* to Part 1 (Base). Part 2 is used with singular nouns, such as *Harriet,* and pronouns such as *he, she,* and *it:*

> Harriet **sips** a hot drink. It **tastes** delicious.

The Part 2 form of *be* is *is:*

> She **is** an accomplished skier.

Past Tense

The past tense, which is used to talk or write about a definite time in the past, is formed by using Part 3 (Past) of a verb. Part 3 of most verbs is **regular** because it is formed by adding the suffix (ending) *-ed* to Part 1 (Base). Part 3 can be used with both singular and plural subjects:

> Two minutes later Leon **placed** his empty cup on the table. Then Harriet **finished** her drink, and they **walked** outside.

Some verbs are **irregular** (not regular) in their Part 3 (Past) forms because they do not add *-ed* to Part 1. You can find these forms in a dictionary by looking for Part 1. Part 3 is shown after Part 1 if the verb is irregular:

Part 1	Part 3	
cut	cut	The wind **cut** through their jackets.
blow	blew	The wind **blew** hard all day.
find	found	Harriet and Leon **found** shelter.

The verb *be* has two forms for Part 3: *was* and *were. Was* is used with singular subjects; *were* is used with plural nouns and pronouns:

Leon **was** happy. They **were** together again.

Future Tense

The future tense is used to discuss or write about something that will happen in the future. It is formed by using Part 1 (Base) of a verb in the following ways:

a. You may use *will* or *shall,* two auxiliary (helping) verbs, with Part 1 (Base) to form the future tense. The auxiliary verb and the main verb together form a unit. *Will* or *shall* and Part 1 of the verb can be used with singular and plural subjects:

Leon **will rent** boots and skis.

b. Another way to write about the future is to use a form of the verb *be* with *going to* and Part 1 (Base) of a verb. In this text, we consider *be going to* + Part 1 as a unit because the whole phrase is needed to express the future tense:

He **is going to take** skiing lessons.

c. Still another way you may show future time is by using Part 1 (Base) or Part 2 (Verb + *s*) of the verb and an adverb telling *when,* such as *next week, later, in a few days, tomorrow:*

Tomorrow Leon **skis** for the first time.

EXERCISE 5C

Read the following paragraph, and notice that it is written in the present tense. Cross out each verb, and write the past tense form above it. The first sentence shows you an example. When you have completed the paragraph, read it with the past tense verbs. Then write the future tense form below each verb. Once more read the entire paragraph, and note the change in perspective.

posed

Portable kerosene heaters ~~pose~~ a threat to home users. One reason is that

will pose

many of these heaters are not vented. As a result, deadly carbon monoxide fills a room. The silent killer easily overcomes unsuspecting people in the room. The kerosene heaters are also a fire hazard. Very hot parts of the heater and the flame frequently ignite papers, curtains, or any other flammable material near them. A third danger is to small children who touch or fall on the heaters. The hot metal burns them badly.

Clearly portable kerosene heaters are not safe for indoor home use.

EXERCISE 5D

Write three sentences. Use the verb tenses indicated in parentheses.

1. (Present)

2. (Past)

3. (Future)

Show these sentences to your instructor or tutor.

The Perfect Tenses

The perfect tenses are used to talk or write about different times in the past or about completion of an activity in the future. (*Perfect* refers to action completed prior to a fixed point of reference.) These tenses are formed by using the auxiliary verbs *have, has,* or *had* with Part 4 (V-ed) of a verb.

Like Part 3 (Past), Part 4 (V-ed) may be regular or irregular. Part 4 of some verbs adds *-ed* to Part 1, but others may show spelling changes:

	Part 1 (Base)	Part 2 (Verb + *s*)	Part 3 (Past)	Part 4 (V-ed)
Regular Verbs	happen	happens	happened	happened
	talk	talks	talked	talked
Irregular Verbs	set	sets	set	set
	sit	sits	sat	sat
	ride	rides	rode	ridden
	choose	chooses	chose	chosen
	am, are, be	is	was, were	been
	have	has	had	had

If you cannot decide whether a verb is regular or irregular while you are writing, look up the base word in a dictionary. If the verb is regular, only Part 1 will appear. If the Part 3 and Part 4 forms are spelled the same, dictionaries usually list the word once. If Part 4 is spelled differently from Part 3, the dictionary will give you Part 4 after Parts 1 and 3. For example, if you look up the verbs *begin* and *buy,* you will find the following forms:

> begin   began, begun
> buy   bought

a. The **present perfect tense** connects an event beginning in the past with the present time. It is formed by using Part 4 (V-ed) with *have* for plural subjects and the pronoun *I; has* is used with singular subjects:

> Leon and Harriet **have waited** two hours for a table in the dining room. (They began waiting two hours before, and they are still waiting.)

b. The **past perfect tense** indicates a time in the past before another time in the past. It is formed by using *had* with Part 4 (V-ed):

> The head waiter **had promised** them a table in one hour. (The waiter had made the promise before Leon and Harriet began waiting for the table.)

c. The **future perfect tense** indicates the completion of an activity in the future. It is formed by using *will have* or *shall have* with Part 4 (V-ed):

> By this time tomorrow Harriet and Leon **will** finally **have gotten** their table.

The following is a time line showing the simple and perfect tenses and the relationship of the tenses to the times the tenses express:

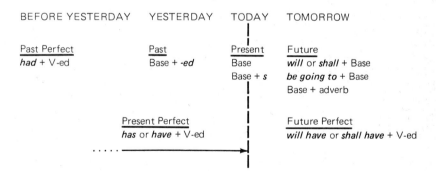

BEFORE YESTERDAY	YESTERDAY	TODAY	TOMORROW
Past Perfect	Past	Present	Future
had + V-ed	Base + *-ed*	Base	*will* or *shall* + Base
		Base + *s*	*be going to* + Base
			Base + adverb
	Present Perfect		Future Perfect
	has or *have* + V-ed		*will have* or *shall have* + V-ed

EXERCISE 5E

Read **all** of the sentences in the exercise below before filling in the blanks. They are about events taking place at different times. Use the verb given in parentheses as the main verb, and add auxiliary verbs if they are needed to show the sequence of events.

1. *(plan)*   Johann and Hilda Zimmer _____ their move to the
                United States for over a year.

2. *(apply)*   Both of them _____ for jobs as managers of a ski
                resort in the United States.

3. *(save)*   They _____ money for the trip for three years.

4. *(arrive)*   Finally the day _____ for the long-distance move.

5. *(say)*   Sadly they _____ goodbye to friends.

6. *(miss)*   Hilda still _____ some of her friends.

7. *(have)*   Johann _____ no regrets.

8. *(enjoy)*   He _____ his job as manager of the ski resort in New
                Hampshire.

9. *(become)*   In a few years Hilda and Johann _____ American
                citizens.

10. *(save)*   By this time next year they _____ enough money
                for a trip home.

The Progressive Tenses

The progressive tenses show something in progress or continuing for a period of time.
They are formed by using Part 5 (V-ing) with forms of the verb *be* as the auxiliary
verb: *am, is, be, are, was, were,* and *been:*

   a. Present: The dog **is barking** again tonight.

   b. Past: He **was barking** last night.

   c. Future: Neighbors **will be yelling** soon.

   d. Present perfect: They **have been complaining** about the dog. (They began com-
                         plaining last week, and they are still complaining.)

   e. Past perfect: Several neighbors **had been talking** to the owner about the dog.
                         (The neighbors had talked to the owner before they began com-
                         plaining.)

   f. Future perfect: By this evening the dog **will have been barking** every night for
                         a week.

Notice that both the V-ed (Past Participle) and V-ing (Present Participle, Gerund) **must
be used with auxiliary verbs** in order to function as verbs in sentences.

EXERCISE 5F

A verb is given in the parentheses before each of the following sentences. Read the sentence. Then write the appropriate form of the verb in the blank, using one of the progressive tenses.

EXAMPLE: (*be* + *test*) Michael _____ is testing _____ the new motorcycle.

1. (*be* + *work*) Donna and Rick _____ at Harry's Drive-in.

2. (*have* + *be* + *study*) The marine biologists _____ water snakes in the area for two years.

3. (*will* + *be* + *fly*) Thousands of people _____ to Europe this summer.

4. (*be* + *run*) The air conditioning unit _____ without problems for a change.

5. (*will* + *have* + *be* + *play*) By this time next year Tom Henry _____ _____ with the baseball league for three years.

6. (*have* + *be* + *ride*) Marilyn _____ her bicycle to work every day.

7. (*will* + *be* + *tape*) Bruce _____ all of the senator's speeches during the tour.

MODAL (ONE-FORM) VERBS

Will and *shall,* used to form the future tense, are two of several verbs called *modal* or *one-form* verbs. **They always function as auxiliary verbs in a verb phrase:**

> *Not:* Leon and Harriet **might** a ski lift up the mountain.
> *But:* Leon and Harriet **might take** a ski lift up the mountain.

Modal (one-form) verbs may be used with a form of *have* and Part 4 of a verb or *be* and Part 5 of a verb:

> They **could have skied** back to the lodge. They **should be watching** for avalanches.

Modal (one-form) verbs help express people's mood or attitude toward something. The modal auxiliaries are words such as *can, could, may, might, shall, should, will, would, must,* and *ought to.*

EXERCISE 5G

You have learned that the verb in a sentence may be a single word or a combination of auxiliary verbs and a main verb. Read each of the following sentences, and underline the verb or verb phrase. Then write the auxiliary verb(s) in the first blank and the main verb or a single verb in the second blank. Do **not** include *not* or *never* in the verb phrase.

	AUXILIARY VERB(S)	MAIN VERB
EXAMPLE: Exercise programs for senior citizens are becoming more common.	are	becoming
Seniors find exercise beneficial.		find

1. In the past older people did not appreciate the value of exercising. _____ _____

2. They simply spent more and more hours in a favorite armchair. _____ _____

3. More recently seniors have been seeing a doctor for a regular checkup. _____ _____

4. As a result, many seniors are taking their pulse regularly. _____ _____

5. Specialists on aging have frequently recommended regular exercise for seniors. _____ _____

6. However, they should not exercise beyond their physical capabilities. _____ _____

7. The exercise programs may include more than physical activity. _____ _____

8. Some groups meet weekly and discuss various aspects of aging. _____ _____

9. In the future some seniors' groups are going to stage special events, such as a Senior Olympics or health fair. _____ _____

SUBJECT-VERB AGREEMENT

Verbs must agree with their subjects in order to keep point of view consistent and thus make writing cohesive. You can say that the subject and verb agree (or are in harmony with each other) when you use one form of a verb with a singular subject and another form of a verb with a plural subject. You have to make this decision for only two tenses—present tense and present perfect tense. For all other tenses you may use the same form of the verb for both singular and plural subjects. If you do not use the verb forms in the ways discussed in this lesson, you may have subject-verb agreement problems in your writing. You may find the correction symbol *SV Agr* to indicate places in your paper where the subjects and verbs do not agree. You can eliminate these problems by being sure that you use the correct form of the verb with singular and plural subjects.

Singular Subjects

Use Part 2 (Verb + *s*) or *has* with Part 4 (V-ed)

1. when the subject is a singular noun or pronoun:

   Sarah explores caves.

2. when the subject is a singular pronoun such as *neither, each, somebody,* or *one:*

   Neither has thought of a solution.

3. when a singular subject is followed by a phrase beginning with *together with, along with, as well as, besides,* and *in addition to:*

   Ketchup as well as mustard **tastes** good with hot dogs.

4. when two or more singular subjects are joined by *or* or *nor* because each noun is considered separately:

   Either **ice plant** or **rosemary makes** a satisfactory ground cover.

Plural Subjects

Use Part 1 (Base) or *have* with Part 4 (V-ed)

1. when the subject is a plural noun or pronoun:

   Oil **paintings cover** the walls of Jonathan's room.

2. when the subject is a plural pronoun such as *they, both, many, few,* and *several:*

   Several have earned the award.

3. when the subject is one or more nouns or pronouns:

   Sam and **Hilary drive** sports cars. **He** and **she have** the same kind.

Singular or Plural Subjects

1. When a sentence begins with the words *there* or *here,* the verb agrees with the subject that follows:

> There **are** several **snapshots** of Miranda.   (snapshots are . . .)
> Here **is** my favorite **one.**   (my favorite one is . . .)

2. The pronouns *any, all, none,* and *some* may take Part 1 (Base) or Part 2 (Verb + *s*):

> **Any** of the contestants **are** eligible. **None are** winners yet.
> **Any** of the information **is** correct. **None is** badly **written.**

3. When two subjects, one singular and one plural, are joined by *either . . . or* or
neither . . . nor, the verb agrees with the noun nearer to it:

> Neither **Mrs. Dominguez** nor her **sisters believe** the strange story.
> Either the **sisters** or **Mrs. Dominguez intends** to talk with the neighborhood gossip.

4. When a collective noun representing a group is considered to be acting as a unit,
Part 2 (Verb + *s*) is used:

> The **band is practicing** today. The **faculty is attending** the rehearsal.

When the members of the group are considered to be acting individually, the base
form of the verb is used:

> The **band have forgotten** their instruments. The **faculty are attending** a meeting.

5. When the subject appears to be plural but represents a unit, Part 2 (Verb + *s*) is used:

> **Ham and eggs is** my favorite breakfast.

When the subject is plural and does not represent a unit, Part 1 (Base) is used:

> **Ham and eggs have** both **gone** up in price.

EXERCISE 5H

Underline each subject and verb in the following sentences. Write the subject in the
first blank and the verb in the second blank. If the verb does not agree with the subject, write the preferred form in the second blank.

	SUBJECT	VERB
1. Each of the pilots have his own headset.	_____	_____
2. You and Tina are our representatives.	_____	_____
3. Reed or Grover is coming to sell tickets.	_____	_____

	SUBJECT	VERB
4. The group of golfers intend to travel by car.	_____	_____
5. None of Dave's friends like his haircut.	_____	_____
6. Shari and Elaine conducts art classes.	_____	_____
7. Neither Brad nor his brother have a job.	_____	_____
8. The supervisor as well as the employees attend training meetings.	_____	_____
9. *The Warriors* is a thrilling movie.	_____	_____
10. The team go to their homes after the game.	_____	_____
11. One of the players have not appeared yet.	_____	_____
12. Either Sylvia or her sisters owns the lot.	_____	_____
13. Five dollars seem reasonable for the repair.	_____	_____
14. Mathematics present no trouble for Janet.	_____	_____
15. There is the suitcases for the trip.	_____	_____
16. The dog in addition to the cats make noise all night.	_____	_____
17. Here is a tent, fishing poles, and bait.	_____	_____
18. Everybody want a pay increase.	_____	_____
19. The floors in the house needs carpeting.	_____	_____
20. Any of these tools are ready for sale.	_____	_____

EXERCISE 5I

Read **all** of the sentences in the exercise below before filling in the blanks. They are about events taking place at different times. One event may have happened in the past, another at a time in the past before another time in the past, and so on. The adverbs help tell you when each event happened. Use the verb given in parentheses as the main verb, and add auxiliary verbs if they are needed. Then write one, two, or three words in the blank. Look at the examples in the lesson if you need help.

Every year crowds of music lovers (1. *gather*) _____ for the
Black Point Music Festival on the outskirts of the city. Many (2. *attend*) _____
_____ since the Festival's beginning ten years ago. Before that, they (3. *travel*)
_____ almost three hundred miles to another state for the musical
festivities. For several years they (4. *discuss*) _____ the possibility of
having the Festival near home. Finally they (5. *choose*) _____ the
present site. The setting at Black Point (6. *be*) _____ in a grove of
oak trees near rolling hills. People (7. *sit*) _____ on bales of hay.
Some (8. *bring*) _____ food to eat. Others (9. *buy*)
_____ barbecued chicken and hot dogs. This year musicians
(10. *play*) _____ music from two stages at the same time. The
Festival organizers (11. *provide*) _____ open areas for people to
dance. Everyone (12. *expect*) _____ to have another successful
Festival.

ASSIGNMENT: Verb Tenses

Write a paragraph about an event or a project that began at a definite time in the past.
Then add details about happenings before the definite time in the past. Next, tell
something about the event in the present. Finally, explain what will happen in the
future. Use as your topic an event or project you understand well. You might, for example, write about an automobile accident; or you might choose a project you
worked on. Label the assignment *Verb Tenses,* and hand it in to your instructor.

Unit 1

Review

You have learned in Unit 1 to use four of five ways to make your writing cohesive: reference, substitution, ellipsis (omission), and meaning. In the first lesson you learned to use specific terms to add details to a general term and to refer to that general term. In Lesson 2 you discovered that you can repeat necessary terms to tie sentences together and that you should delete (omit) unnecessary words.

Lesson 3 showed you ways to make writing cohesive by using adjectives to make general terms specific and to extend the meaning of general terms. It also showed how to use adverbs to tie sentences together in time relationships. You practiced combining several sentences by taking adjectives from some sentences and placing them in a base sentence to extend the meaning of general terms. In Lesson 4 you learned to use pronouns to refer to preceding nouns and to substitute pronouns for nouns in order to avoid needless repetition.

Lesson 5 on verb tenses helped you relate ideas together in a time sequence and maintain a consistent point of view by using subject-verb agreement.

Now you can apply all these techniques to the exercises in this review.

When you complete this Unit 1 Review, check your answers with your instructor's answer key.

IA. Organizing General and Specific Ideas
(16 points—2 points each)   SCORE _____

The following list contains information for a paragraph about limitations color-blind people face. Following the list are sentences that develop the information.

First, make an outline for yourself by organizing the items in the list below in the order in which they should appear in the paragraph. Use numbers 1, 2, 3, and so on to show the levels of generality.

List of ideas for a paragraph on   Your outline
color-blind people

___1___ Limitations color-blind people
            face
a. _____ Unqualified for certain jobs
b. _____ Pilots—colored signal lights and
            flags
c. _____ Two limitations
d. _____ Traffic officers and truck
            drivers—red/green traffic signals
e. _____ Needing help in organizing a
            color-coordinated wardrobe
f. _____ Choosing one basic color for a
            wardrobe and matching accessories
g. _____ Interior decorators and paint
            salespeople—colors for decora-
            tion
h. _____ Numbering outfits and placing
            corresponding numbers on
            matching accessories

IB. Organizing Sentences for a Paragraph
       (16 points—2 points each)   SCORE _____

Using the outline you developed about color-blind people, organize the sentences below into a paragraph. Write the paragraph in the space provided.

a. Color blindness limits people in at least
   two ways.
b. For example, pilots must respond to
   colored signal lights and flags.
c. First, color-blind people may not be
   eligible for certain jobs.
d. Interior decorators and paint salespeople must be very sensitive to different shades of the same color.
e. Second, color-blind people can cope
   with the limitation in planning a color-
   coordinated wardrobe in two ways.

f. Or they can have someone mark each accessory with a number to match the number of each outfit.

g. Anyone driving, such as traffic officers and truck drivers, must tell the difference between red and green traffic lights.

h. Either they can wear one basic color and match all accessories to it.

II. Combining Sentences
(48 points—3 points each)   SCORE _____

Read each of the following sets of sentences. Place X before the base sentence. Draw a line through the unnecessary words in the remaining sentences. Then insert the modifiers in the base sentences. Add punctuation wherever it is needed. Write your combined sentences below the sets.

1. The travelers were searching for adventure.
   There were five travelers.
   They were bored.
   They were grouchy.
   They were searching for an unusual adventure.

2. Their trip lacked excitement.
   The trip was three weeks long.
   The trip was cross-country.
   The trip was in an automobile.

3. The driver turned the car down a road.
   The driver was curious.
   The road was unpaved.
   The road was abandoned.

4. The passengers began to see signs.
   The passengers were excited.
   The signs were broken.
   The signs were weather-beaten.
   The signs were along the road.

5. The signs advertised a ride.
   The signs were faded.
   The ride was inexpensive.
   The ride was scenic.
   The ride was one hour.
   The ride was in an airplane.

6. The travelers found the airfield.
   They were happy.
   The airfield was run-down.
   The airfield was in a shallow valley.
   The airfield was near a river.

7. The pilot collected their money and helped them into the plane.
   The pilot was smiling.
   The pilot was bearded.
   The plane was old.
   The plane seated six passengers.

8. The plane taxied down the runway.
   The plane was creaking.
   The plane was a single-engine plane.
   The runway was dusty.
   The runway was unpaved.

9. The passengers gripped their seats as the plane left the ground.
    The passengers were white-faced.
    The plane was rattling.

10. The pilot banked suddenly.
    The pilot was grinning.
    The bank was to the left.

11. He flew low.
    The flying was over some trees.

12. The passengers stared out the windows at the river below.
    The passengers were nervous.
    The windows were dirty.
    The river was sparkling.

13. The flight finally ended with a landing.
    The flight was frightening.
    The landing was bumpy.

14. The passengers climbed out of the plane.
    The passengers were perspiring.

15. Then the passengers talked about the flight.
    They were relieved.
    The flight had been exciting.

16. The travelers wanted an adventure.
    They were smiling.
    The adventure would be new.

III. Revising a Paragraph
   (20 points—1 point each)   SCORE _____

The following paragraph is organized satisfactorily, but the paragraph is not cohesive
because point of view changes several times. You will find problems with pronoun-
antecedent agreement, pronoun reference, verb tenses, and subject-verb agreement.
Read the entire paragraph. Then cross out words to be changed, and write the revisions
above them.

Most people want soft, wrinkle-free skin. Therefore, you buys creams and lotions

for your face and body. First, you spends money for bleaches to remove "age spots."

Then the same people spends even more money for tanning lotions, and you stay in

the hot sun for hours. The results was inevitable. Skin became dry and sometimes

looked like leather. The dryness then made the skin wrinkle. Severely sun-damaged

skin can later develop skin cancer. We can keep skin soft by taking certain precautions.

We should limit exposure to the sun. She can protect the face with a large-brimmed

hat and wears clothes with long sleeves over her arms. They can also use sun-screen

lotions. The lotions scatters or blocks the ultraviolet light of the sun. A few precau-

tions saved people from sun-damaged skin.

Unit 2

Sentence Transitions and Connectors

Basketball players in an action-filled game move fluidly from one end of the court to the other in ever-changing patterns, one team striving to put the ball into its basket despite blocking by the other team. It is only after long hours of practice before games that a team can quickly make moves that place members in advantageous positions for scoring additional points. With experience and continuing practice a team learns to work together as a unit and stays the winner.

You have been using four of the five techniques—reference, substitution, ellipsis, and meaning—in single sentences to make your writing as fluid and cohesive as the movements of the basketball players. In this unit you will study the fifth technique—using connectors to tie sentences together. By practicing sentence connecting and combining, you will learn to remove obstacles to understanding from your readers' paths and to produce sentences that let your readers move effortlessly from one point to another.

If you write a series of sentences with no connection between them, you force your readers to provide the connections. In some cases the readers may relate ideas in a way that changes the meaning of what you intend to express. As a result, you are not communicating effectively with your readers. In the example that follows, the first set of sentences gives information about wind as an alternative source of energy, but understanding clearly what the writer has to say is difficult because the sentences seem to jump back and forth from one aspect of the topic to another. In the second set, the same sentences have been connected and combined to show the relationship of ideas:

Electricity, natural gas, and oil have been used as sources of energy for homes and industries. People in this century have ignored the power of the wind as another source of energy. Less natural gas and oil are now available. People have come to recognize the wind as an important source of energy. Researchers have been developing efficient windmills. The windmills can generate electricity for houses. The windmills can run deep well irrigation pumps for hundreds of acres of farmland.

Because electricity, natural gas, and oil have been used as sources of energy for homes and industries, people in this century have ignored the power of the wind as another source of energy. **However, now that** less natural gas and oil are available, people have come to recognize the wind as an important source of energy. **As a result,** researchers have been developing efficient windmills that can generate electricity for houses and run deep well irrigation pumps for hundreds of acres of farmland.

To provide logical connections between sentences you write, you will learn to connect and combine two or more sentences, examining first how the ideas in them are related to one another and then trying a variety of ways to show the relationships. You will study the following relationships of ideas in Unit 2: addition (Lesson 6); time (Lesson 7); cause, result, purpose (Lesson 8); comparison (Lesson 9); concession, manner, condition (Lesson 10); alternation (Lesson 11); and emphasis, enumeration, summation (Lesson 12). These lessons will also cover the connectors that express these relationships and the punctuation to use with them. The entire list of connectors and the relationships they express are summarized in Lesson 13.

Of the millions of words in the English language only a small number function as connectors. They are easy to identify because they do not change their spelling and they cannot take endings. Connectors may be words that function as prepositions, words such as *to, in, on, by, because of,* and *under,* which you studied in Lesson 3; or they may be conjunctions such as *and, but, until,* and *when,* and conjunctive adverbs such as *however* and *nevertheless.* Although each kind of connector has its own name, you do not have to remember the names, but you will have to know how each kind functions in sentences, partly because each kind is used with certain punctuation. To help you become familiar with the words in each of the three groups, each kind will be printed as they are shown in the examples that follow:

Coordinating conjunctions
   printed in capital letters and underlined: AND, BUT, FOR, OR, NOR, YET

Conjunctive adverbs
   printed in small letters and underlined: however, then, in addition

Subordinating conjunctions
   printed in capital letters: BECAUSE, WHEN, IF, UNTIL, ALTHOUGH

In the lessons that follow you will learn to determine the relationship of ideas between and among sentences and to use connectors to express the relationships.

Lesson 6

Addition

Drivers traveling along streets and roads usually follow the rules they have learned, but they also respond to signs and signals along the way. A speed limit sign, for example, tells them how fast to travel on a road, a pedestrian crossing sign warns them to watch for people in a crosswalk, and a stop sign tells them to come to a complete stop before proceeding through an intersection.

Your readers respond to the rules and patterns of written language when they read. However, like the drivers, they need signals to help them understand the relationship of ideas in a set of sentences or a paragraph. You learned in lessons in Unit 1 to give your readers signals with, for example, pronoun reference, repetition of terms, and specific terms that elaborate on general terms. In this lesson you will learn to strengthen the connection between and among sentences by using the following connectors, which may be used to show that one sentence adds information to another sentence:

COORDINATING CONJUNCTION	CONJUNCTIVE ADVERBS
AND	furthermore
	in addition
	moreover
	also
	again
	besides
	too

DETERMINING THE RELATIONSHIP OF IDEAS

Before you join two or more ideas with the connectors listed above, you should decide, first, whether the second idea actually gives additional information about the first one. Look for repetition of terms, specific terms that elaborate on general terms, and pronouns that refer to nouns, techniques of cohesive writing you studied in Unit 1. When you read the following sentences, you can see that they are not related to one another. The first one is about the County Council members and complaints, the second about Holden Reinhardt and his position, and the third about employees and a pay raise:

The County Council members heard complaints about a proposed shopping center.
Holden Reinhardt is chairman of the board of State Savings Bank.
The employees accepted the 10 percent pay raise.

Now as you read each of the following pairs of sentences, you can see that each second sentence is related to the sentence before it by repetition of terms and pronoun reference. In the first pair, for example, *members* appears in both sentences. In the second pair, *He* in the second sentence refers to Holden Reinhardt in the first sentence and thus connects the second sentence to the first one. In each pair, the second sentence adds information about the problems, situations, or happenings in the first sentence. You can test the relationship by inserting *also* in the second sentence. If the second sentence adds information, *also* will in many cases fit logically in the sentence:

> The County Council members heard complaints about a proposed shopping center. The members (also) authorized a sewer system for a new subdivision.

> Holden Reinhardt is chairman of the board of State Savings Bank. He is (also) the manager of the Crystal Chemical Company.

> The employees accepted the 10 percent pay raise. It (also) included increased health benefits.

In sentences that are not connected by pronoun reference or repeated terms, you can determine whether the second sentence gives additional information by looking for words in each sentence that express similar or related ideas. In the following example the connection between the sentences is expressed by words such as *Pierre* and *two other people, volunteer* and *donated,* and *teacher* and *school:*

> Pierre worked one hundred hours as a volunteer teacher. Two other people (also) donated their time to the school.

EXERCISE 6A

Read each of the following pairs of sentences. If the second sentence gives information that can be added to the first sentence, write A in the blank at the right. Look for repetition of terms, pronoun reference, and related terms. In many cases you can insert *also* in the second sentence. If the second sentence does not add information to the first sentence, write X in the blank.

EXAMPLE: Florence Smith received a car from her parents on her college
              graduation day.
              Her uncle thought she was too young to own a car.   X

              Florence grew fond of her car.
              She relied on it to take her everywhere.   A

1. Florence looked at her car's speedometer one day several years later.
    She examined the paint carefully.

2. The ten-year-old green Maverick had small nicks on the left door.
   A long, narrow dent from a falling brick marred the door on the right. _____

3. The car did have a few problems over the years.
   Florence took care of the problems as they appeared. _____

4. One problem was a leaking radiator hose.
   The brakes seemed unreliable at times. _____

5. More recently oil was leaking into the radiator.
   Car owners should plan for regular maintenance. _____

6. Florence thought about all the stalled cars she had passed along the
   freeway.
   She considered herself to be lucky. _____

7. She had driven the car across the United States one summer.
   She made weekly trips from her home to San Francisco. _____

8. Florence shopped for a used car.
   She looked at new cars. _____

9. Eventually she found a silver Buick with low mileage at a reasonable
   cost.
   Her old Maverick seemed like a faithful friend. _____

10. Finally, she sold the Maverick to a young man who liked to repair
    cars.
    The Buick has proved to be dependable. _____

LINKING SENTENCES WITH CONNECTORS

Once you have decided that the second sentence gives additional information about
the first sentence, you can use a connector in the second sentence to express addition
and thus make your writing cohesive. The connector functions as a transition (*trans*
means *across*) or a "bridge" by carrying the idea from the first sentence to the second
sentence.

Connectors that function as transitions are conjunctive adverbs such as <u>further-
more</u>, <u>in addition</u>, and <u>moreover</u>. They may appear at the beginning of the second
sentence or within the second sentence. Because they are transitions, they are not a
part of the sentence; therefore, they are enclosed in commas:

> The County Council members heard complaints about a proposed shopping center.
> **In addition,** the members authorized a sewer system for a new subdivision.

> *Or:* The members authorized, **in addition,** a sewer system for a new subdivision.

Adverbs such as *also, again, besides,* and *too* may function as transitions to link
sentences:

Holden Reinhardt is chairman of the board of State Savings Bank. **Besides,** he is the manager of the Crystal Chemical Company.

When these adverbs function as adverbial modifiers within the sentences or at the end of sentences, no commas enclose them:

Holden Reinhardt is chairman of the board of State Savings Bank. He is the manager of the Crystal Chemical Company **besides.**

EXERCISE 6B

The sentences in this exercise are the same ones you worked with in Exercise 6A. In this exercise add a connector that expresses addition to each second sentence that adds information to the first sentence. Refer to your answers in Exercise 6A to identify the sentences.

EXAMPLE: Florence Smith received a car from her parents on her college
            graduation day.
            Her uncle thought she was too young to own a car.   ___X___

            Florence grew fond of her car.
            Moreover, she relied on it to take her everywhere.   ___A___

1. Florence looked at her car's speedometer one day several years later.
   She examined the paint carefully.   _____

2. The ten-year-old green Maverick had small nicks on the left door.
   A long, narrow dent from a falling brick marred the door on the right.   _____

3. The car did have a few problems over the years.
   Florence took care of the problems as they appeared.   _____

4. One problem was a leaking radiator hose.
   The brakes seemed unreliable at times.   _____

5. More recently oil was leaking into the radiator.
   Car owners should plan for regular maintenance.   _____

6. Florence thought about all the stalled cars she had passed along the
   freeway.
   She considered herself to be lucky.   _____

7. She had driven the car across the United States one summer.
She made weekly trips from her home to San Francisco. _____

8. Florence shopped for a used car.
She looked at new cars. _____

9. Eventually she found a silver Buick with low mileage at a reasonable cost.
Her old Maverick seemed like a faithful friend. _____

10. Finally, she sold the Maverick to a young man who liked to repair cars.
The Buick has proved to be dependable. _____

USING CONNECTORS TO COMBINE SENTENCES

When you connect (fasten together) two separate sentences, each sentence retains its identity; that is, it stays a sentence. The connector serves as a transition, a bridge, between the related ideas:

> Celestia Lincoln found speakers for the counselors' conference. **In addition,** she arranged meals and sleeping accommodations at the hotel.

You can show readers an even closer relationship between the two ideas by combining (blending together) the two sentences into one. To give equal emphasis to each idea in each sentence, you simply tie the sentences together with an appropriate connector. Each sentence is then identified as an independent clause in the new sentence:

> *First independent clause* -
> Celestia Lincoln found speakers for the counselors' conference;
>
> *Second independent clause* -
> **in addition,** she arranged meals and sleeping accommodations at the hotel.

A clause is a word group with a subject and a predicate. It may be either an independent clause or a dependent clause. (You will study dependent clauses in Lesson 7.) If the clause can stand alone as a sentence, it is an independent clause. The difference between a sentence and an independent clause is that a sentence begins with a capital letter and ends with a period, question mark, or exclamation point; the independent clause does not because it functions as a part of a sentence.

Once you have determined that the second sentence in a set gives additional information, you can combine the two sentences with connectors expressing addition. These are the same connectors you used to connect sentences in the preceding part of this lesson: <u>furthermore</u>, <u>in addition</u>, <u>besides</u>, <u>moreover</u>, <u>also</u>, <u>again</u>, and <u>too</u>. You may also add to this list the coordinating conjunction <u>AND</u>.

Before you go further, you should learn the difference between the two kinds of connectors because each functions in a particular way and requires certain punctuation:

COORDINATING CONJUNCTION	CONJUNCTIVE ADVERB
The coordinating conjunction is a two- or three-letter word (AND, BUT, YET, OR, NOR, FOR) that connects two or more coordinate (equal) words or word groups which receive equal emphasis.	The conjunctive adverb is also a connector, but it functions as a transition by carrying an idea from one sentence to another.
It can appear only at the beginning of a sentence when it is connecting two sentences.	It can appear at the beginning of a sentence or within a sentence.

Using the coordinating conjunction AND or conjunctive adverbs, you can combine sentences in any of these three ways:

1. Use a comma and the word **and** (, AND) to connect two independent clauses:

   The County Council members heard complaints about a proposed shopping center, **AND** the members authorized a sewer system for a new subdivision.

2. Use a semicolon (;) alone to combine two independent clauses. In addition, you may use the word **also** in the second clause if you wish:

   Holden Reinhardt is chairman of the board of State Savings Bank; he is (also) the manager of the Crystal Chemical Company.

3. Use a semicolon between two independent clauses. Then insert a connector such as in addition, moreover, also, or besides in the following ways:

   a. Place the connector at the beginning of the second independent clause and use a comma after it:

      The employees accepted the 10 percent pay raise; **in addition,** it included increased health benefits.

   b. Place the connector within the second independent clause. If it functions as a transition, enclose it in commas:

      Holden Reinhardt is chairman of the board of State Savings Bank; he is, **moreover,** the manager of the Crystal Chemical Company.

   c. Place the connector within the second independent clause. If it functions as an adverbial modifier, do not enclose it in commas:

      Pierre worked one hundred hours as a volunteer teacher; two other people **also** donated their time to the school.

To add variety to your sentences, use any of the ways discussed in this lesson to connect and combine your sentences. Because the meanings of the connectors and adverbs differ slightly in certain contexts, you should check the meanings of the words in a dictionary.

EXERCISE 6C

Connect or combine the following pairs of sentences by using connectors such as AND, in addition, moreover, and furthermore. A second choice is to use only a semicolon between two sentences. You may also use adverbs such as again, besides, too, and also. In the following examples the connector to be used appears in slash marks to the left of the sentence in which it is to appear. The punctuation to be used appears between slash marks to the right of the sentence the punctuation is to follow.

EXAMPLE: The rancher raised dairy cows.   /,/
           /**AND**/   He grew the grain to feed the cows.

                  The rancher raised dairy cows, **AND** he grew the grain to
                  feed the cows.

EXAMPLE: The rancher raised dairy cows.   /;/
        /**moreover**/   He grew the grain to feed the cows.

                  The rancher raised dairy cows; **moreover,** he grew the
                  grain to feed the cows.
                  Or: The rancher raised dairy cows; he grew, **moreover,** the
                  grain to feed the cows.

1.   Justin packed his bag for his trip to Philadelphia.   /,/
      /**AND**/   He put the new contracts into his briefcase.

2.   The air express service promises overnight delivery of letters and
                  packages from one office to another.   /;/
    /**moreover**/   It offers the same type of service from hotels to business offices.

3.   Manufactured goods can be transported in cargo planes.
                  They can be transported by trucks and trains.

4.   People in prison can sometimes earn high-school or college credit through correspondence courses.
       In some areas they can earn credit by taking televised courses.

5.   The landlord explained the terms of the rental contract.
       He insisted on a sizeable, nonrefundable cash deposit.

6.   The small shop was lined from the floor to the ceiling with paperback books.
       It featured current best sellers on tables near the door.

7.   The young author sold her first story to a women's magazine.
       She sold a travel article to a local newspaper.

8.   Molly decided not to order a dress from the sales catalog.
       Joan decided not to place an order.

EXERCISE 6D

Write three sentences that show the addition of one idea to another.

1. (AND)

2. (;)

3. (in addition or moreover)

Show these sentences to your instructor or tutor.

COMBINING THREE OR MORE SENTENCES

If three or more sentences are related, you may combine them with one or more connectors that express addition. You begin by examining the relationship of the ideas. Then you determine how you will combine the sentences. In the following example each of the three sentences tells what concerned people did for the homeless old couple and adds further information about the help the couple received:

Single sentences:
After the fire the neighbors gave the homeless old couple clothing and furniture.
News reporters at a television station collected contributions for the couple.
An apartment owner let the couple live in an apartment free of charge for a month.

Combined sentences:
After the fire the neighbors gave the homeless old couple clothing and furniture, news reporters at a television station collected contributions for the couple, **AND** an apartment owner let the couple live in the apartment free of charge for a month.

The sentences are related by repetition of *couple* and the words naming the concerned people: *neighbors, news reporters,* and *apartment owner.* In addition, *gave, collected,* and *let* all indicate help the couple received. When combining three sentences, you can use a comma between the first two sentences instead of AND. Then you can place a comma and AND between the second and third sentences.

EXERCISE 6E

Connect or combine the following sets of sentences. Use connectors that express addition to link the sentences together, or a semicolon alone. Add other punctuation wherever it is needed.

EXAMPLE: Industrialists searched for new ways to improve production. */,/*
    /AND/ They found using robots for certain jobs satisfactory since the early 1960s.

Industrialists searched for new ways to improve production, AND they found using robots for certain jobs satisfactory since the early 1960s.

1.   Today robots perform tasks in the assembling of products.   */;/*
      They load and unload parts and transport them.   */;/*
/in addition/ They are involved in the inspection of finished products.

2.

/also/

In the manufacture of automobiles robots frequently do the
welding.   /;/
The robots / paint cars.

3.

Several furniture makers use robots for planing, shaping, and
finishing wood.
At a plant in Pennsylvania three robots assemble typewriter-ribbon
cartridges.
A motor assembly plant uses robots to screw electric bulbs into instrument panels and assemble parts of an electric motor.

4.

Manufacturers of dangerous chemicals use robots instead of people to
work with the chemicals.
Robots are able to save people from danger by handling radioactive
materials.

5.

In some cases robots can handle the repair of equipment under greater
atmospheric pressure than people can withstand—deep in the ocean,
for example.
Robots can work in a sterile workroom and maintain the sterile
atmosphere better than people can.
They are better able to perform tasks in unsuitable environments
such as high humidity.

6.

Robots can be fitted with special devices that function as a human
arm.
They can pick up parts, drill holes, and insert screws.
Often they take over routine or dangerous jobs.

USING CONNECTORS AS TRANSITIONS
IN PARAGRAPHS

In this lesson you have learned to determine whether ideas in two sentences are related to one another. You have also learned to use connectors that express addition
between two sentences. And you have learned to combine two or more sentences

with related ideas. By connecting some sentences and combining others, you can vary the length of sentences you write in a paragraph. For reports you might write shorter sentences than you write for essays. You will also want to vary sentence length to avoid monotony.

In the following example the first sentence summarizes the paragraph by indicating that the applicant must be qualified for the position:

> The applicant for the executive secretary's position must be well qualified. He or she should have had at least five years' experience as an executive secretary. This experience should include scheduling appointments and trips, transcribing dictations, keeping confidential records, and maintaining an up-to-date client file. **In addition,** the applicant should be able to supervise three other employees, **AND** he or she should be able to interview and hire applicants for any of the three positions. The applicant, **moreover,** should be able to gather information for and edit the weekly employee newsletter.

By using numbers to show the levels of generality, which you studied in Lesson 1, you can examine the relationship of each sentence in the paragraph to the others. The first sentence summarizing the paragraph is level 1. The sentences providing the details about qualifications are all level 2, and the sentences giving more information about the level 2 statements are labeled level 3. Here is the paragraph:

1 The applicant for the executive secretary's position must be well qualified.

    2 He or she should have had at least five years' experience as an executive secretary.

        3 This experience should include scheduling appointments and trips, transcribing dictations, keeping confidential records, and maintaining an up-to-date client file.

    2 **In addition,** the applicant should be able to supervise three other employees, **AND** he or she should be able to interview and hire applicants for any of the three positions.

    2 The applicant, **moreover,** should be able to gather information for and edit the weekly employee newsletter.

The outline shows clearly how using connectors can make your writing cohesive. In other words, the three level 2 statements are linked together by the connectors that show the relationship of the statements.

EXERCISE 6F

The following paragraph has been written without connectors. Read the entire paragraph, and determine how ideas are related to one another. Then insert connectors expressing addition wherever they are needed to combine or connect the sentences. You may refer to the list of connectors expressing addition on page 63. If you are not sure how the ideas are related, you might number the sentences to show the levels of generality. Then you will be able to find the sentences that tell in what ways the shopping mall satisfies most people's needs. Finally, add the necessary punctuation.

The new shopping mall will probably satisfy most people's needs. It has at least a dozen clothing stores with clothes to fit everyone's budget. One shop, for example, sells men's shirts for five dollars. Another sells them for fifty to a hundred dollars. The new mall has three restaurants. Two department stores in the mall each have a restaurant. The artist needing supplies can find them in two shops. Musicians can find musical instruments and sheet music in another shop. Shoppers will want to spend several hours in the mall shops.

ASSIGNMENT: Addition

Write a paragraph in which you have eight to ten sentences in the completed version. Choose a subject that will allow you to use connectors that show addition. You might tell what kinds of training one needs for a job or a sport, what qualifications a person needs for a particular job, or the qualities or characteristics one looks for in making a purchase of merchandise or real estate. Begin by writing down your ideas. Then use connectors such as AND, also, moreover, and furthermore, and modifiers such as besides, again, and too to express addition. After you have connected and combined sentences, add necessary punctuation. Label the paragraph *Addition,* and hand it in to your instructor.

FIRST, NEXT, FINALLY

When you write about more than two events in a sequence, you should first write your sentences in the order in which each event took place. The following example explains three things Lorenzo did, and the sentences are arranged to show the order in which he did them. These sentences might look very much like the notes that you jot down as you think about what you are going to write:

> Lorenzo built the storage shed.
> Lorenzo built it next to the garage.
>
> He moved belongings.
> He moved them from closets.
> He moved them into the shed.
>
> He carefully organized all the belongings.
> He organized them in three locations in the shed.

You can combine these sentences, using the procedure you learned in Lesson 3. First, mark the base sentence with X. Then cross out unnecessary words and insert the remaining words in the base sentence:

> X Lorenzo built the storage shed **/**.
> ~~Lorenzo built it~~ next to the garage.
>
> X He moved belongings **/** .
> ~~He took them~~ from closets **/** .
> ~~He carried them~~ into the shed.
>
> X He carefully organized all the belongings **/** .
> ~~He placed them~~ in three locations in the shed.

The second step, then, is to combine each set of sentences:

> Lorenzo built the storage shed next to the garage.
> He moved belongings from closets into the shed.
> He carefully organized all the belongings in three locations in the shed.

The final step is to combine the sentences by adding connectors such as <u>first</u>, <u>second</u>, <u>third</u>, <u>next</u>, <u>finally</u>, <u>then</u>, and <u>later</u>, all of which tell when each activity took place. A semicolon appears at the end of the first independent clause, and a comma usually follows the connectors. Because <u>then</u> functions more as an adverb than a conjunction in the sentence, you do not need a comma. (Other words that function similarly are <u>still</u>, <u>hence</u>, and <u>also</u>.) The combined sentence follows:

> Lorenzo built the storage shed next to the garage; **then** he moved belongings from closets into the shed; **finally,** he carefully organized all the belongings in three locations in the shed.

EXERCISE 7A

Read all of the following sentences. Then combine є   set of sentences by completing the following steps. Place X before the base sente.   Then draw a line through
unnecessary words, and insert the remaining words in ι   ɔase sentence.

1. Stephanie hired new salespeople.
   The salespeople were for the garden shop.

2. She organized a training program.
   The training program was for the salespeople.
   The training program was for the next week.

3. She asked the manager to conduct the training program.
   The manager worked in the garden shop.

4. She prepared practice exercises.
   The exercises were for operating the cash register.

After you have combined the sentences, connect or combine the new set of sentences
above about Stephanie with connectors that show a time relationship—first, second,
third, next, finally, then, and later.

Show these sentences to your instructor or tutor.

EXERCISE 7B

Write at least five sentences showing a sequence of events. You may write about preparations for something, the sequence of events in an accident, or the procedure for doing something. Show the time relationship by connecting and combining your sentences with connectors such as first, second, third, next, finally, then, later, and still later.

Show these sentences to your instructor or tutor.

SUBORDINATING CONJUNCTIONS AND DEPENDENT ADVERBIAL CLAUSES

Up to this point you have been combining sentences by using two kinds of connectors—coordinating conjunctions (AND) and conjunctive adverbs (in addition, moreover, furthermore), and you have studied the punctuation used with each kind. Both of these connectors join coordinate ideas—ideas on the same level—expressed in two or more independent clauses.

The third kind of connector is the subordinating conjunction, words such as BEFORE, AFTER, WHEN, WHILE, and AS. Here is a comparison of the subordinating conjunction and the conjunctive adverb, such as furthermore and in addition:

SUBORDINATING CONJUNCTION	CONJUNCTIVE ADVERB
It can appear only at the beginning of a clause.	It can appear at the beginning of a clause or sentence or within a clause or sentence.
It functions as a connector, combining two clauses—one dependent, the other independent.	It functions as a transition between independent clauses or within a sentence.
It changes an independent clause to a dependent clause.	It does not change an independent clause.
Only commas separate dependent clauses from independent clauses. No commas enclose the subordinating conjunction.	A semicolon appears between two independent clauses. Commas enclose the conjunctive adverb.

The dependent clause, as its name indicates, cannot stand alone because it is a fragment, a part of a sentence. It must be attached to an independent clause. The following example shows a sentence first and then the same words changed to a dependent clause beginning with AFTER:

> *Sentence:* Brett had made the decision to sell his horse.
> *Dependent Clause:* **AFTER** Brett had made the decision to sell his horse

The idea in the dependent clause is subordinate to (of lesser rank than) the idea in the independent clause. A dependent clause beginning with a subordinating conjunction may be called a subordinate clause or an adverbial clause, and it functions as an adverb in the sentence. Adverbial clauses can appear at the beginning, in the middle, or at the end of sentences.

> **AFTER** Brett had made the decision to sell his horse, he suddenly changed his mind.
> Brett, **AFTER he had made the decision to sell his horse,** suddenly changed his mind.
> Brett suddenly changed his mind **AFTER he had made the decision to sell his horse.**

BEFORE, AFTER, WHEN, WHILE, AS

In order to use a subordinator, or any other connector, accurately, you should think consciously about the meaning of the word or check the meaning in a dictionary. The following examples show how you can change the meaning of a combined sentence with different subordinators. You can also change the emphasis by making first one sentence, then the other, the independent clause in the combined sentence. You can begin with two sentences:

> The furniture auction began.
> Cristina tried to find her friend in the enormous crowd.

When you use AFTER, you show that one event happened first and another second, and you emphasize Cristina's search for her friend. When you combine the two sentences, you must change the past tense verb *began* to *had begun,* the past perfect tense (Lesson 5) to show that Cristina's search for her friend took place after the auction had begun:

> **AFTER** the furniture auction had begun, Cristina tried to find her friend in the enormous crowd.

If you use BEFORE to join the sentences, you change the meaning completely. The first sentence emphasizes Cristina's search; the second one emphasizes the beginning of the auction:

> **BEFORE** the furniture auction began, Cristina tried to find her friend in the enormous crowd.

> The furniture auction began **BEFORE** Cristina tried to find her friend in the enormous crowd.

You can show that both events happened at the same time by using AS and WHILE:

> **AS** the furniture auction began, Cristina tried to find her friend in the enormous crowd.
> **AS** Cristina tried to find her friend in the enormous crowd, the furniture auction began.
> **WHILE** Cristina tried to find her friend in the enormous crowd, the furniture auction began.

You can use WHEN to indicate a particular time or moment that something happened:

> **WHEN** the furniture auction began, Cristina tried to find her friend in the enormous crowd.

Two more connectors that can be used to combine the pair of sentences are SINCE and UNTIL. SINCE in the following sentence means "from the time that" the auction had begun. UNTIL in the second example means "up to the moment that" the auction began:

> Cristina tried to find her friend in the enormous crowd **SINCE** the furniture auction had begun.

> Cristina tried to find her friend in the enormous crowd **UNTIL** the furniture auction began.

Punctuation with Dependent Clauses
Introduced by Subordinating Conjunctions

When a dependent clause telling when something happened appears at the beginning of a sentence, it is followed by a comma:

> **WHEN** the bricklayer stumbled, he twisted his ankle.

If the dependent clause appears within the sentence, it is enclosed in commas:

> The bricklayer, **WHEN** he stumbled, twisted his ankle.

When the dependent clause appears at the end of the sentence, no commas are used:

> The bricklayer twisted his ankle **WHEN** he stumbled.

EXERCISE 7C

Combine the following sets of sentences by using connectors that show time and addition relationships. You may use any of the following connectors with suitable punctuation: <u>AND</u>, AFTER, BEFORE, WHEN, WHILE, AS, <u>first</u>, <u>next</u>, <u>finally</u>, and others. In the blank at the right write either *Time* or *Addition* to indicate the relationship the connector expresses. In the example and the first two sentences in the exercise the connectors are given before the sentences, and the punctuation to be used appears at the end of the sentence.

EXAMPLE: Some students panic.
          /BEFORE/   They take an exam.   _____ Time _____

                      Some students panic BEFORE they
                      take an exam.

1. /AS/   Their heartbeat increases.   /,/   _____

             They get a stomachache or a headache.   /,/
   /AND/   They cannot focus their eyes.   _____

2.   Workshops about test anxiety help students cope
             with stress.
   /BEFORE/ They are faced with an exam.   _____

3.   Students' anxiety about exams is reduced.
             They attend the workshop.   _____

4.   Some stress is beneficial.
             It does not prevent the student from functioning. _____

5.   Students become too relaxed.   _____
             Students do not care how they perform on the
             exams.

6.   Students should follow several steps.
             They receive the exam.   _____

7.   They should read the directions twice.   _____
             They should underline the important parts of the
             directions.   _____
             They should review all the questions to discover
             the easy ones.   _____

ASSIGNMENT: Time

Write a paragraph of eight to ten sentences about an event that takes place over a period of time. You might write about moving to a new place or beginning a new job. Use connectors and modifiers between and within sentences to indicate time and addition. Label the paragraph *Time,* and hand it in to your instructor.

Cause, Result (Effect), Purpose

Having studied the connectors you can use to express addition and time in Lessons 6 and 7, you should begin to see that you can change the meaning of the same pair of sentences by using first one connector and then a different connector between them, depending on the meaning you want to convey. In other words, knowing how to use these connectors accurately enhances your skill as a writer. Not only can you write well-constructed, individual sentences, but you can also relate ideas logically to one another and thus make your writing cohesive and easily understandable for your readers.

In this lesson you will study the following connectors and learn to use them to express cause, result (effect), and purpose:

	COORDINATING CONJUNCTION	CONJUNCTIVE ADVERB	SUBORDINATING CONJUNCTION
Cause	FOR		BECAUSE SINCE
Result	AND (therefore)	consequently as a result thus therefore then hence	
Purpose			SO THAT IN ORDER THAT

CAUSE OR REASON

Sentences that give a reason or a cause for something consist of two parts: a statement giving a result preceded or followed by a second statement that tells the cause or reason why something happened:

Result:	The nine-year-old girl stopped reading. (Why?)
Cause/Reason:	She had heard a noise in the next room.

Result:	She was afraid to investigate. (Why?)
Cause/Reason:	She might find someone in the next room.

You help your readers understand the reason by placing the second idea in a dependent clause beginning with BECAUSE, which must be combined with the independent clause into a single sentence:

> The nine-year-old girl stopped reading **BECAUSE** she had heard a noise in the next room. She was afraid to investigate **BECAUSE** she might find someone in the next room.

You cannot use BECAUSE to introduce the first sentence in each pair above because they do not give the cause/reason. The combination would be illogical:

> *Not:* **BECAUSE** the nine-year-old girl stopped reading, she had heard a noise in the next room. **BECAUSE** she was afraid to investigate, she might find someone in the next room.

"She was afraid to investigate" was a result in the pair of sentences above. In the next pair of sentences it becomes the cause/reason in relation to the second sentence. In combining the pair you can give the cause/reason first:

Cause/Reason:	She was afraid to investigate.
Result:	She covered her head with her sweater.

> **BECAUSE** she was afraid to investigate, she covered her head with her sweater.

If someone asks you in conversation why you want to quit your job, you may answer, "Because I need a change." In conversation such an answer is satisfactory because the person asking the question has supplied the first part of a statement, and you have responded with a second part. Both of you understand the two parts of the idea expressed. In writing, however, you must combine a "because" answer, a fragment, with an independent clause. BECAUSE is a subordinating conjunction, a connector that makes a clause dependent on another clause:

> *Not:* I want to quit my job. **BECAUSE** I need a change.
> *But:* I want to quit my job **BECAUSE** I need a change. (No punctuation after *job*)

A connector you can use in place of BECAUSE is SINCE:

> **SINCE** I have not received a raise, I plan to quit my job.
> **SINCE** prices have risen dramatically, most people must limit the amount they buy.

As you learned in Lesson 7, you punctuate dependent clauses beginning with subordinating conjunctions in the following ways: A dependent clause at the beginning of the sentence is followed by a comma. A dependent clause within the sentence is enclosed in commas. No comma appears before a dependent clause at the end of the sentence.

Still another connector that tells why is <u>FOR</u>, a coordinating conjunction, which connects two independent clauses. Remember that punctuation consists of a comma before the coordinating conjunction:

> The retired police officer volunteered to help children at the busy intersection, **FOR** he needed something to keep him active.

EXERCISE 8A

Combine the following sentences in these steps. First, read each pair of sentences, and write *Cause/Reason* after the sentence that tells why. Then use one of the connectors that express cause or reason—BECAUSE, SINCE, and <u>FOR</u>—before the sentence giving the reason, and write the combined sentence after the letter *c.* Next, read each pair again to determine which ones might show a time relationship. Then use connectors such as AFTER, WHEN, BEFORE, AS, WHILE, or UNTIL to combine the sentences. Write the second combined sentence after the letter *d.* If you cannot show a time relationship, leave the space blank.

EXAMPLE: a. Jon hired a private plane to take him across the mountains.
b. He had to attend a meeting in three hours.   **Cause/Reason**
c. Jon hired a private plane to take him across the mountains **BECAUSE** he had to attend a meeting in three hours.
d.

a. Jon was ordered to appear at the home office.   **Cause/Reason**
b. He left the branch office immediately.
c. **SINCE** Jon was ordered to appear at the home office, he left the branch office immediately.
d. **AFTER** Jon was ordered to appear at the home office, he left the branch office immediately.

1a. The security guard cleaned his gun carefully.
 b. He wanted to be ready at all times.
 c.

 d.

2a. Sandra likes to eat strawberries.
 b. She has planted fifty strawberry plants in her garden.
 c.

 d.

3a. The car stopped suddenly.
  b. A small dog chased a black cat across the road.
  c.

  d.

4a. Harley had fertilized the orange trees carefully.
  b. They produced more oranges than usual that season.
  c.

  d.

5a. Maria's new car rusted quickly the first winter in Minneapolis.
  b. Snow removal crews had used salt on the roads.
  c.

  d.

EXERCISE 8B

Write three sentences in which you use BECAUSE, SINCE, or <u>FOR</u> as connectors between two ideas.

1. (BECAUSE)

2. (SINCE)

3. (<u>FOR</u>)

Show these sentences to your instructor or tutor.

RESULT OR EFFECT

As you learned in the first part of this lesson, you can write a sentence identifying a cause or a reason for something. Then you can match that sentence with a second one that gives the result or effect, and you use BECAUSE, SINCE, or <u>FOR</u> to connect the sentences. Another way to show the relationship is to combine the two sentences, using connectors such as <u>consequently</u>, <u>as a result</u>, <u>thus</u>, <u>therefore</u>, <u>then</u>, and <u>hence</u>, all of which indicate result:

Single sentences:

Cause: Sara-Jean and Rick both drive recklessly.
Result: They have each been involved in at least five accidents.

Cause: Snowfall in the mountains was below normal last winter.
Result: Water volume in the river is below normal this summer.

Combined sentences:

Sara-Jean and Rick both drive recklessly; **consequently,** they have each been involved in at least five accidents.

Snowfall in the mountains was below normal last winter; **as a result,** water volume in the river is below normal this year.

You may also find that you will use <u>AND</u> as a connector and the word ***therefore*** in the second part of the sentence:

Cause: Steve Wilson was late for the buyers' meeting.
Result: He lost the sale.

Steve Wilson was late for the buyers' meeting, **AND** he therefore lost the sale.

Before you begin the following exercise, review Lesson 6 to refresh your memory about punctuation you use with coordinating conjunctions and conjunctive adverbs.

EXERCISE 8C

In the following exercise you have the same pairs of sentences that you worked with in Exercise 8A. This time read both sentences, and then label the cause and the result. Finally, combine them by using connectors such as <u>consequently</u>, <u>as a result</u>, <u>thus</u>, <u>therefore</u>, <u>then</u>, <u>hence</u>, and <u>AND</u> (therefore). Add punctuation where it is needed:

EXAMPLE: Jon had to attend a meeting in three hours.   _____Cause_____
He hired a private plane to take him across the
mountains.   _____Result_____

Jon had to attend a meeting in three hours; **consequently,** he hired a private plane to take him across the mountains.

1. The security guard wanted to be ready at all times. _____

   He cleaned his gun carefully. _____

2. Sandra likes to eat strawberries. _____

   She has planted fifty strawberry plants in her garden. _____

3. A small dog chased a black cat across the road. _____

   The car stopped suddenly. _____

4. Harley had fertilized the orange trees carefully. _____

   They produced more oranges than usual that season. _____

5. Snow removal crews had used salt on the roads. _____

   Maria's new car rusted quickly the first winter in Minneapolis. _____

EXERCISE 8D

Write three sentences in which you show a cause in the first part and the result in the second part. Use connectors given in the parentheses.

1. (consequently)

2. (as a result)

3. (therefore)

Show these sentences to your instructor or tutor.

PURPOSE

To show the reason or purpose for doing something, you can use SO THAT and the modal (one-form) verbs *could, should, would, may,* or *might* (Lesson 5) in the second part of the sentence. The modal verb indicates that the purpose is suggested—that the people hope to protect their homes—but that the purpose might not be carried out:

Single sentences:

The people planted trees on the west side of their houses.
Purpose: They wanted to protect their homes from the afternoon sun.

Combined sentences:

The people planted trees on the west side of their houses
Purpose: **SO THAT** they might protect their homes from the afternoon sun.

The same two sentences can show a cause relationship. The sentence with the verb *wanted* expresses the people's reason why they planted trees:

The people planted trees on the west side of their houses
Cause: **BECAUSE** they wanted to protect their homes from the afternoon sun.

If you use <u>as a result</u> between the two sentences, you change the meaning again, this time telling your readers that the people succeeded in protecting their homes:

The people planted trees on the west side of their houses;
Result: **as a result,** they protected their homes from the afternoon sun.

You can change the meaning of the following pair of sentences in the same way:

Single sentences:

The child pushed the chair to the table.
He would be able to reach the cookie jar.

Combined sentences:

The child pushed the chair to the table
Purpose: **SO THAT** he would be able to reach the cookie jar.

The child pushed the chair to the table
Cause: **BECAUSE** he wanted to reach the cookie jar.

The child pushed the chair to the table;
Result: **as a result,** he was able to reach the cookie jar.

EXERCISE 8E

Write two sentences that show purpose. Connect the ideas with SO THAT.

1.

2.

Show these sentences to your instructor or tutor.

EXERCISE 8F

Read each of the following sets of sentences. Decide whether the relationship shown in the sentences is cause, result, or purpose; and write *cause/reason, result,* or *purpose* in the blanks at the right. Then combine the sentences by using an appropriate connector.

1. Oil is needed in the automobile engine.
   It reduces wear caused by friction.   _____

2. The oil must be changed at regular intervals.
   Engine wear is not accelerated.   _____

3. Old oil is loaded with acids, dirts, and abrasives.
   An oil sludge forms.   _____

4. How often to change oil is a difficult question to answer.
   So much depends on how the automobile is used.   _____

5. Oil sludge is most likely to form in a car engine that seldom
   reaches highway speed.   _____
   The engine does not become hot enough to burn off moisture
   in the crankcase.

6. A delivery car that drives in town seldom reaches a high speed. _____
   The oil must be changed frequently.

7. Many companies that use delivery cars change the oil every _____
   sixty days.
   The operating life of the car will be increased.

8. Synthetic oils reduce engine friction. _____
   They increase gasoline mileage.

ASSIGNMENT: Cause, Result, Purpose

Write a paragraph in which you have eight to ten sentences in the completed version. Choose a subject that will allow you to use connectors that express cause/reason, result, and purpose. For example, you might tell the reasons why a problem exists and the results caused by the problem. Or you may show the purpose for some action and the results or causes connected with it. You might write about the causes for or the results of the success of a particular program or the causes for losing a job; the results (effects) of air conditioning or of pesticides; the purpose for building a strong defense system or for developing synthetic fuels. Begin by writing down your ideas and then organizing them. Develop sentences. Then use connectors such as BECAUSE, SINCE, FOR, consequently, as a result, thus, therefore, then, hence, IN ORDER THAT, and SO THAT to connect and combine sentences. Include any other connectors you need to make your paragraph cohesive. Finally, add necessary punctuation. Label the paragraph *Cause, Result, Purpose,* and hand it in to your instructor.

Lesson 9

Comparison: Similarity, Difference, and Contrast

Including comparisons in your paragraphs or essays makes them cohesive because you examine a person, object, or idea in relation to another. Comparison helps determine whether they are similar or different and makes you aware of specific characteristics of whatever you are comparing. Suppose, for example, that people in your neighborhood have decided to set aside a particular piece of land for a community park. You and others believe that another site is preferable. What arguments can you present to convince the others to agree with you? You and members of your group can list what you believe are characteristics of a desirable piece of property for a park. Then you can compare each piece of land with the characteristics you have listed to decide which of the two sites is the better one. Even if you finally decide that the first piece of property is preferable, you will feel satisfied because you have examined each site in detail and matched it with characteristics you feel a good park site should have.

COMPARISON OF TWO PARCELS OF LAND

Desired characteristics	Land A	Land B
Central location in park district	Centrally located	At east edge of park district
Transportation—easily accessible by bus	Served by five bus routes	Served by one bus route
Size of area—five to ten acres	Four acres	Ten acres
Trees—at least one grove of 20 trees per acre	One grove	Three groves—many individual trees
Land contour—flat or slightly rolling	Flat	Four acres flat, six acres rolling
Water supply—local water district and natural streams	Water district line	Water district line, small stream through middle of land

From this comparison you can prepare a written report, explaining why one piece of land is recommended instead of the other.

First, you make a statement that explains what you intend to compare. This statement serves as a topic sentence for a paragraph. Then you match the characteristics of each person or item you are comparing. In comparing Land A and Land B as possible park sites, examine details that show similarities and differences. If you set the details in opposition to one another, you then emphasize the differences and show how they contrast with one another:

> The neighbors on Birch Avenue have matched the desired characteristics for a community park with those of Land A and Land B and have decided that Land B is much more suitable as a park site **THAN** Land A. It is true that Land A is centrally located and offers more bus service **THAN** Land B, **BUT** the other characteristics of Land B make it the preferable park site. One favorable characteristic of Land B is the six acres of rolling land. The small hills will act as accoustical barriers to keep the noise level down. Another advantage is the small stream running through the middle of the land. Possibly the stream can be dammed later to create a small lake. Most important is the acreage and the number of trees. Land B is two and a half times larger **THAN** Land A and has probably three times **AS** many trees **AS** Land A. Land B should accommodate the residents for a longer period of time **THAN** Land A, **AND** the three groves of trees will provide more picnic areas **THAN** the single grove on Land A. Obviously Land B would be a much better park site **THAN** Land A.

For comparisons and contrasts to be valid, you have to examine characteristics in an orderly manner. In this lesson you will study the modifiers and connectors that express similarity and contrast:

	COORDINATING CONJUNCTION	CONJUNCTIVE ADVERB	SUBORDINATING CONJUNCTION
Similarity		similarly likewise in the same way also too	AS AS . . . AS
Contrast	BUT AND	on the one hand on the other hand nevertheless however on the contrary instead in comparison	THAN

SIMILARITY

Conjunctive adverbs such as similarly, likewise, in the same way, also, and too can connect two ideas that are similar. You may use the words to combine sentences or to provide transitions between them. Notice that the punctuation is the same as the punctuation that you learned to use with other conjunctive adverbs:

Single sentences:
The managers and buyers in the department store want a raise.
The salespeople want a raise.

Combined:
The managers and buyers in the department store want a raise; the salespeople **also** want
a raise. *or* . . . the salespeople want a raise **too.**

Single sentences:
Many parents expect their children to share household duties with them.
The children expect their parents to treat them fairly.

Combined:
Many parents expect their children to share household duties with them; the children
in a similar way (similarly) expect their parents to treat them fairly.

Connected with a transition:
Many parents expect their children to share household duties with them. The children
in a similar way (similarly) expect their parents to treat them fairly.

The word AS or the combination AS . . . AS can also be used to show similarity. You
will see that some words are repeated in the single sentences, but they can be understood when the two sentences are combined. Punctuation used with AS and AS . . . AS
is the same as that used with other subordinating conjunctions:

Single sentences:
Joan has plans for the study center.
Mel has the same plans for the study center.

Combined:
Joan has the same plans for the study center **AS** Mel (does). *or*
Joan's plans for the study center are the same **AS** Mel's (plans are).

Single sentences:
Joan is enthusiastic about her plans.
Mel is enthusiastic about his plans.

Combined:
Joan is **AS** enthusiastic about her plans **AS** Mel is about his (plans).

You can express similarity by using *both, same,* or *similar* in a single sentence about
two people, objects, or ideas. These words function as pronouns or modifiers; they
are not conjunctions:

Both men drive Corvettes and wear toupees.
In addition, they have **similar** extensive wardrobes.
They **also** drink the **same** kind of wine—cream sherry.

EXERCISE 9A

Combine the following sentences to show similarity between the two ideas. For some sentences you can use similarly, likewise, in the same way, also, or too between the two parts. When words are repeated in the second sentence, use AS or AS . . . AS. Examine the examples that follow, and review other examples in this lesson. Use appropriate punctuation wherever it is needed.

EXAMPLE: Steven showed exceptional courage in saving the drowning child.
Margaret ignored her own safety when she fought a fire in the neighbor's house.

Steven showed exceptional courage in saving the drowning child; **in a similar manner,** Margaret ignored her own safety when she fought a fire in the neighbor's house.

EXAMPLE: Gordon enjoys cross-country skiing very much.
His brother enjoys cross-country skiing.

Gordon enjoys cross-country skiing **AS** much **AS** his brother does.

1. Jeff collects and classifies old coins.
   His brother collects and classifies stamps.

2. People on the east side of the river are enthusiastic about the new marina for their boats.
   People on the west side of the river are enthusiastic about the new marina for their boats.

3. Katie needs much help with her math problems.
   Victor needs much help with his math problems.

4. The clothing manufacturing company is hiring fifty people.
   The furniture factory is hiring fifty people.

5. The Blue Streak Auto Club members followed the same route through the mountains.
   The Gasohol Gang followed the same route through the mountains.

EXERCISE 9B

Write three sentences that show the similarities between two or more people, objects, or ideas, using the connectors in parentheses.

1. (also)

2. (similarly)

3. (AS . . . AS)

Show these sentences to your instructor or tutor.

DIFFERENCE

When two people, objects, or ideas are different from one another, you can indicate the difference by using THAN to show the comparison:

> *Single sentences:*
> The apples on this tree are sweet.
> The apples on that tree are sweet.
>
> *Combined:*
> The apples on this tree are sweeter **THAN** those on that tree (are sweet).

In addition to using THAN, you also have to add *-er* to *sweet* to make it the comparative form of the adjective. If an adjective consists of two or more syllables, you probably should use *more* or *less* before it (some two-syllable words such as *handsome* or *scary* take the *-er* suffix—*handsomer, scarier*):

> This campaign seems more organized **THAN** that one (does).
> That campaign seems less likely to succeed **THAN** that one (does).

You also add *-er* or use *more* or *less* with adverbs in comparisons:

> Sabrina files cards faster **THAN** the other clerks in the department.
> The senator speaks more convincingly **THAN** the representative.

When you compare two characteristics of the same person, you show the comparison between two adjectives instead of between the subjects of the two sentences. In the next example the comparison is between *sympathetic* and *critical:*

> Nina is usually more sympathetic **THAN** critical when people tell her their troubles.

Because you are combining two sentences when you make a comparison, you have to watch the form of pronouns after THAN. In the following example, the subject form *I* appears after THAN because it is the subject of the second clause:

> *Single sentences:*
> Gino likes to play tennis
> I like to play tennis.
>
> *Combined:*
> Gino likes to play tennis better **THAN** I (like to play tennis).

If you compare three or more people, objects, or ideas, use the superlative degree of the adjective which you form by adding *-est* to the one- or two-syllable adjectives. With the longer words use *most* and *least:*

> Jacques is the happiest person in the group.
> These three houses are the most attractive ones on the street.

EXERCISE 9C

To each of the following sentences add an idea that shows a difference between the one given and the one you add. Use suitable connectors. Refer to the examples in the lesson for possible patterns.

EXAMPLE: Traffic is heavy on Route 49.
            Traffic is **heavier** on Route 49 **than on Route 75.**

1. Tropical plants require water.

2. A motorcycle engine is loud.

3. Reggie is responsible.

4. Jackson Construction Company builds houses quickly.

5. Our dog likes my brother.

Show these sentences to your instructor or tutor.

EXERCISE 9D

Write four sentences that show the difference between two or more people, objects, or ideas. Use the forms of modifiers indicated in the parentheses. Review examples given in this lesson.

1. (Add the *-er* suffix to the adjective or adverb.)

2. (Use *more* before the adjective or adverb.)

3. (Add the *-est* suffix to the adjective or adverb.)

4. (Use *most* before the adjective or adverb.)

Show these sentences to your instructor or tutor.

CONTRAST

To emphasize differences, you can contrast the differences with one another by using BUT and the conjunctive adverbs on the one hand, on the other hand, on the contrary, instead, in comparison, however, and nevertheless between sentences. The punctuation is that used with conjunctive adverbs:

> **On the one hand,** Nelson talks about getting a college degree; **on the other hand,** he prefers to be free to travel.

> Nelson can continue to waste his own time; **however,** his father will not let him waste money, especially money he has not earned.

> Tomatoes and oranges grow abundantly in California's hot, dry Central Valley; **in comparison,** lettuce and artichokes grow only along the coast where sea breezes provide needed moisture and moderate temperatures.

You can also use BUT to show contrast:

> The candidate for the senate seat attacked the welfare program, **BUT** he could not offer a realistic alternative to help needy people.

BUT can show contrast between two verbs, adjectives, or adverbs:

> Sonia **refused** the offer at first **BUT** finally **accepted.**
> The house is **comfortable** in the summer **BUT cold** in the winter.
> Teddy climbed the tree **quickly BUT carefully.**

EXERCISE 9E

Combine the following sentences to show contrast. Use any of the following connectors to join the sentences: BUT, on the one hand, on the other hand, on the contrary, instead, in comparison, however, and nevertheless.

1. Steve had planned to work as an accountant.
   He is a hospital administrator.

2. The adventure movie promised to be the best of the year.
   It is one of the most poorly made films ever produced.

3. The tomatoes in the greenhouse should have produced fruit by now.
   They are only sprawling vines.

4. Sylvia enjoys most pets.
   She cannot stand cats near her.

5. The Johnsons have saved money for a trip for years.
   They never seem to find the time for travel.

WRITING A COMPARISON OR A CONTRAST

Whether you write a paragraph or an essay to show comparison and contrast, your preparation for the writing is essentially the same. First, write down all the points you intend to compare. Then match them with one another carefully.

TOPIC: Comparison of videocassettes and videodiscs

Similarities:
Both store electronically recorded images that can be projected on television screens.

Differences:

Characteristics	Videocassettes	Videodiscs
Size	Smaller but thicker	Larger but thinner
Storage space required	Smaller storage space	Larger storage space
Cost	Double that for video-disc	Half the cost of video-cassette
Playback equipment	Videocassette recorder	Videodisc player
Cassettes/discs	Blank cassettes available for recording TV programs or making home movies	Blank discs not available
	Cassettes reusable	Discs not reusable
	Commercially recorded cassettes twice the cost of discs	Commercial recorded discs half the cost of cassettes

Look over your list to decide whether the comparisons are about the same thing. When you are satisfied that all points are in order, you are ready to write your comparison. Begin with a topic sentence (a thesis statement for an essay) that names the two or more people, objects, or ideas to be compared. Next, give examples of similarities. Finally, explain the differences. The order of the details depends on the emphasis you want to place on the ideas expressed and on the weight of evidence on either side. The following paragraph, an example of a comparison, explains the similarities and differences between videocassettes and videodiscs:

Buyers interested in purchasing motion pictures, variety shows, and sports programs for home viewing on their television sets have to decide whether to purchase the programs on videocassettes or videodiscs. In comparing these electronic storage units, buyers discover that **both** the videocassettes and videodiscs can store the **same** electronically recorded images. As they investigate further, they find differences. For example, they learn that videocassettes are smaller **but** thicker **THAN** videodiscs. Videocassettes look like small rectangular boxes, about the size of a pound of margarine, **BUT** videodiscs are thin and round like long-playing phonograph records. As a result, storage cabinets for each kind must be **different.** The costs **also** differ. Prerecorded videocassettes cost at least twice **AS** much **AS** the videodiscs. Buyers **also** learn that cassettes and discs require **different** playback equipment. Videocassette players cost twice **AS** much **AS** the videodisc players **but** offer the buyers more flexibility because buyers can purchase blank cassettes and record television programs themselves; in addition, they can purchase a videocamera for making home movies. **In contrast,** buyers cannot purchase blank discs. Buyers who believe that videodiscs produce sharper television pictures **THAN** videocassettes probably choose videodiscs instead of videocassettes. Having examined the similarities and differences between videocassettes and videodiscs, buyers can make a choice to suit their personal preferences.

EXERCISE 9F

Write a comparison in which you explain similarities and differences, being careful to complete each part of the comparison before going on to the next one. Given below are details that compare owning a house or a condominium. Read through them carefully. If you do not understand any of the points, discuss them with your instructor. Then write a topic sentence for the paragraph. You may compare the similarities and differences. You may explain why owning a house gives people more advantages than owning a condominium. Or you may explain why owning a condominium gives more advantages than owning a house. Before you write the paragraph, show the topic sentence to your instructor or tutor.

TOPIC: Owning a house or a condominium

Similarities:

Save money (build equity) by investing in home ownership
Income tax deduction of real estate taxes
Control over interior decoration

Differences:

House	Condominium
Yard upkeep or gardener	No yard upkeep—possible maintenance fee
Privacy in yard for outdoor activities	Communal yard
Cost of installing and maintaining pool	Pool, tennis court, racquet ball court, sauna, exercise room

When you have completed your paragraph, show it to your instructor or be prepared to hand it in to your instructor.

ASSIGNMENT: Comparison

Write a paragraph of eight to ten sentences in the completed version. Compare and contrast two or more people, objects, or ideas. You may, for example, compare cameras, heating systems, cartoon characters, life-styles, techniques of two artists, sports events, and so on. Label the assignment *Comparison,* and hand it in to your instructor.

Lesson 10

Concession, Manner, and Condition

In Lesson 9 you examined two ideas to decide whether they were similar to each other or whether they were in contrast with each other by comparing them. Such a comparison makes a paragraph cohesive because you are examining a person, object, or idea in relation to another. In the following examples the first sentence shows similarity between two laws, and the second one shows the difference in the cost of houses in two areas:

Similarity: The proposed hiring practices law is **AS** discriminatory **AS** the present one.
Difference: Houses in Los Angeles are more expensive **THAN** those in Fresno.

In this lesson you will also be comparing two ideas, but this time you will be studying relationships other than similarity and difference. The first relationship is concession, acknowledgment that one idea contrasts with or opposes another idea. The second relationship is manner, which tells how one thing is done in comparison to something else. And the third is condition, which shows the possibility that something might be done. By using the following connectors, you will be able to show these relationships and connect or combine sentences:

	COORDINATING CONJUNCTIONS	CONJUNCTIVE ADVERBS	SUBORDINATING CONJUNCTIONS
Concession	YET BUT	nevertheless however admittedly to be sure	ALTHOUGH THOUGH EVEN THOUGH WHILE WHEREAS
Manner			AS AS IF AS THOUGH
Condition			IF PROVIDED THAT UNLESS

CONCESSION

In studying contrast in Lesson 9, you learned to show an idea in the first part of a sentence opposing an idea in the second part by using connectors such as <u>BUT</u> or <u>on the contrary</u>:

> Dale entered the marathon, **BUT** he did not expect to win.
> Fritz, **on the contrary,** expected Dale to take first prize.

In sentences showing concession (or acknowledgment), you also express ideas that oppose one another; but the idea expressed in the second part is contrary to what one would expect and, in some cases, may be a surprise. For example, the first part of the following sentence indicates Dale should be able to win the marathon:

> Dale has spent many hours training for the marathon.

The readers expect to learn in the next part of the sentence that Dale has a good chance of winning because he has been training. Instead the second part expresses an idea contrary to what the readers expect, and it concedes that Dale may not be able to win the marathon even though he has been in training:

> Dale has spent many hours training for the marathon, **YET (BUT)** he lacks the necessary stamina and determination to win.

The following is another example illustrating how the connectors introduce a second idea that admits that the first part of the statement can be accepted only with certain limitations:

> *Single sentences:*
> The sun is beneficial to humans as a source of Vitamin D.
> Too much sun can eventually cause skin cancer.

> *Combined:*
> The sun is beneficial to humans as a source of Vitamin D; **YET** too much sun can eventually cause skin cancer.

> The sun is beneficial to humans as a source of Vitamin D; **however,** too much sun can eventually cause skin cancer.

> **ALTHOUGH** the sun is beneficial to humans as a source of Vitamin D, too much sun can eventually cause skin cancer.

The connectors WHEREAS and WHILE indicate an acknowledgment of contrast between similar ideas:

> The land north of the river has a very high grain yield per acre **WHEREAS (WHILE)** the land south of the river scarcely produces enough to cover costs.

You can use <u>admittedly</u> and <u>to be sure</u> to acknowledge a view that opposes yours:

> **Admittedly,** cigarette smoking fulfills a need of the smoker, but smoking must be limited to certain areas to protect the non-smoker from pollution caused by the cigarette smoke.

Punctuation used with each of the connectors—coordinating conjunctions, conjunctive adverbs, and subordinating conjunctions—is the same as that in Lessons 6 and 7 and summarized in Lesson 13.

EXERCISE 10A

Combine the following pairs of sentences by using one of the following connectors to show concession: <u>YET</u>, <u>BUT</u>, <u>however</u>, <u>nevertheless</u>, ALTHOUGH, THOUGH, or EVEN THOUGH. Include necessary punctuation (Lesson 13).

1. Many people think of caves as muddy tunnels.
   Caves may actually contain huge caverns hundreds of feet high and streams.

2. Most exploring in a cave is done by walking.
   The memorable parts are climbing over boulders, swimming in the lakes or streams, and squeezing through narrow places.

3. Generally cave "squeezes" are fairly short in length.
   Many cave explorers are frightened by tight spaces in caves.

4. People of all sizes explore caves successfully.
   Confident, thin cavers have an advantage in tight spaces.

5. Seventy years ago people explored caves with only a candle for light.
   Today a miner's electric cap-lamp provides the light.

EXERCISE 10B

Write sentences using the connector in parentheses after each number. Include necessary punctuation (Lesson 13).

1. (YET)

2. (however)

3. (nevertheless)

4. (ALTHOUGH)

5. (WHEREAS or WHILE)

Show these sentences to your instructor or tutor.

MANNER

You can use adverbs to tell in what manner (how) someone moves or acts or how something is done:

> The little girl sipped her drink slowly.   (How? slowly)

You can also tell how her father acted:

> Her father sipped his drink slowly.

Then you can put the two sentences together to compare the manner in which the girl and her father sipped their drinks, using AS to combine the sentences:

> The little girl sipped her drink slowly **AS** her father did.

Such a comparison as the one above is literal because it compares the actions of two human beings—the little girl and the father. Because they are both human beings, they are in the same class. Here are more literal comparisons about the actions of two people. The first example compares Joel's actions to those of his father. The second example compares the way Faria's grandmother cooked with the way Faria now cooks. The part beginning with AS tells how, and it means *in the same way that.* You can also use *just* or *exactly* before AS to emphasize the similarity:

Single sentences:
Joel swaggers and swears.
His father swaggered and swore.

Combined:
Joel swaggers and swears **AS** his father did.
              . . . in the same way that his father did.

Single sentences:
Faria's grandmother cooked a meal outdoors in a large pot.
Faria cooks a meal outdoors in a large pot.

Combined:
Faria's grandmother cooked a meal outdoors in a large pot just **AS** Faria does now.

You can also write literal comparisons of animals and objects:

The puppy sits up and begs for food just **AS** its mother does.
The new car operates exactly **AS** the old one did.

In the next example, the sentence gives a comparison of the actions of two beings—a boy and a pony. The comparison this time is figurative because the boy and the pony are in two different classes—human being and animal. AS shows similarity between the two ideas and means *in a manner similar to:*

The carefree young boy streaked through the woods **AS** a pony might.
              . . . in a manner similar to that of a pony.

The next comparison is also figurative because the writer compares a person with an animal and supposes that the swimmer's movement through the water is like that of an otter. You can use AS IF or AS THOUGH to tell how something looks or someone acts or appears. *Were* used with *she* indicates that the second part of the statement is not a fact—she is not an otter. The verb indicates the second part is hypothetical (imagined):

The well-trained swimmer glided through the water **AS IF** she were an otter.

In the next sentence, the comparison is literal, and the part following AS IF is a fact:

She swims **AS IF** (or **AS THOUGH**) she has trained herself well.

EXERCISE 10C

Read each of the following sentences and determine which one of the following relationships each sentence expresses by writing the letters A, B, C, or D in the blanks at the right. Review examples in the lesson if you need help.

Literal comparison: A. in the same manner   B. a factual statement
Figurative comparison: C. in a manner similar to   D. an imagined situation

1. The new student tries to act as if she were an authority on Shakespeare. _____

2. The man-made marble looks as if it were real marble. _____

3. The baritone in the barbershop quartet sings as if he were a frog. _____

4. Dan's face looks as if he stayed in the sun too long. _____

5. Myra styles her hair as a professional hairdresser might. _____

6. Carson mixes and applies colors to the canvas as his teacher taught him to do. _____

7. The worn tire looks as if it should be replaced. _____

8. The children float in the water as air mattresses might. _____

9. The woman in the floor-length dress glides as if her feet were well-oiled wheels. _____

10. The teenager speaks softly as his father does. _____

EXERCISE 10D

Write two sentences in which you use connectors to show manner or tell how something looks or someone acts or appears. Use examples in the lesson as patterns for your sentences.

1. (AS)

2. (AS IF or AS THOUGH)

Show these sentences to your instructor or tutor.

CONDITION

Connectors used to express condition are IF, PROVIDED (THAT), and UNLESS. When you use IF alone, you are indicating that one situation, or sometimes more than one, depends on the existence of another situation. The following sentences indicate two situations—first, agreeing to terms and, second, signing the contract:

> *Single sentences:*
> The employees agree to the terms.
> They will sign the contract.

The first idea, stated as a separate sentence, seems to indicate that the employees have actually reached an agreement. However, they may not have arrived at that point. To show that the idea in the first sentence is a possibility, but not yet a reality, you can place IF before the sentence. IF means *on condition that . . . :*

> *Combined:*
> **IF** the employees agree to the terms, they will sign the contract.
> *On condition that* the employees agree . . .

You can use PROVIDED (THAT) to show condition more forcefully. It means *only if . . .* in the following example:

> **PROVIDED THAT** the employees agree to the terms, they will sign the contract.
> *Only if* the employees agree . . .

Another word that shows condition is UNLESS. It connects a statement about a problem or concern to another statement that shows under what conditions the problem or concern will be resolved:

> The employees will not sign the contract **UNLESS** they agree to the terms.
> The employees will walk out tomorrow **UNLESS** the company meets their demands.

The next sentences, which include the same information about the employees and their contract, show other relationships with connectors you have studied:

Time:	**WHEN** the employees agree to the terms, they will sign the contract.
Time:	**AFTER** the employees agree to the terms, they will sign the contract.
Cause:	**SINCE** the employees agree to the terms, they will sign the contract.
Cause:	The employees will sign the contract **BECAUSE** they agree to the terms.
Addition:	The employees agree to the terms, **AND** they will sign the contract.

EXERCISE 10E

Combine the following pairs of sentences by using IF, PROVIDED (THAT), or UNLESS as the connector.

1. People who are blind can learn to play the guitar easily.
   The teacher adapts lessons to meet their needs.

2. Blind players can judge the position of their fingers on the finger board of the guitar.
   They learn to make use of the guitar's physical cues.

3. Blind students usually progress as rapidly as sighted students.
The instruction for locating finger positions has been poor.

4. The blind guitarist may practice at home.
The lesson is available in a non-visual medium.

EXERCISE 10F

Write sentences using the connectors given in parentheses after each number.

1. (IF)

2. (PROVIDED THAT)

3. (UNLESS)

Show these sentences to your instructor or tutor.

EXERCISE 10G

Fill in the blanks in the following paragraph with connectors that indicate time, purpose, result, and condition. Use the chart on pages 124-26 to help you recall the connectors you have studied.

A lost hiker has excellent chances for surviving in the wilderness (1) _____ he uses common sense and does not panic. Fright, desperation, exhaustion, and shock are the greatest danger to the hiker (2) _____ he does not stay calm. (3) _____ the hiker realizes he is lost, he should sit down and relax (4) _____ he listens for sounds and thinks about what they might be. (5) _____ he must prepare a shelter (6) _____ he will be relatively warm and comfortable (7) _____ he must spend the night in the wild. (8) _____ the hiker prepares his shelter, he should gather wood for a fire. Big pieces of wood are better than scraps (9) _____ big pieces burn longer. (10) _____ no one has found the lost hiker by the next day, he can add green leaves to the fire to produce smoke. He should not wander too far from his camp (11) _____ his rescuers may not be able to find him.

ASSIGNMENT : Concession, Manner, and Condition

Write a paragraph of about eight to ten sentences in the completed version. Use connectors that indicate concession, manner, and condition. Look again at the list of these connectors given at the beginning of this lesson. Choose a subject that allows you to examine conditions under which something might be accomplished and explain the manner in which conditions might be met. You might write about a contract a group is considering or the conditions under which a competition might take place. Include any other connectors you need to make your paragraph cohesive. Label the paragraph *Concession, Manner, and Condition,* and hand it in to your instructor.

Lesson 11

Alternation

Whether you are aware of it or not, you spend a good part of your time making choices. You choose when you will get up in the morning, what you will eat, what you will wear, and how you will spend your free time. You also have choices in planning long range goals—whether you will change jobs, take a trip, buy a car, be friends with someone. You can help your readers make choices by using your choice in a particular situation as an example of a possible choice.

To present the choices or alternatives in a clear, easily understandable pattern, you can explain first one choice and then another. To show the relationship of these ideas and make your writing cohesive, you can use the following connectors between ideas or sentences:

COORDINATING
CONJUNCTIONS

OR
NOR

USING OR AS A CONNECTOR

When you have finally saved enough money for a vacation, you may choose one of two places where you can entertain yourself for that amount of money. In talking or writing about these choices, you can first list them:

I can hike in the mountains for two weeks.
I can spend a weekend in San Francisco.

If you combine these possible choices into a single sentence, you can indicate that each one is an alternative by using OR as the connector. A comma follows the first independent clause and then OR:

I can hike in the mountains for two weeks, **OR** I can spend a weekend in San Francisco.

You might also indicate your choices by using <u>BUT</u> to contrast one choice with the other:

> I have enough money to hike in the mountains for two weeks, **BUT** I can use that money instead for a weekend in San Francisco.

If, however, you use <u>AND</u> instead of <u>OR</u>, you indicate to your readers that you have enough money for both activities:

> I can hike in the mountains for two weeks, **AND** I can spend a weekend in San Francisco.

<u>OR</u> indicates that only one choice is possible:

> Carlos can live in the single-family house himself, **OR** he can rent it to someone else.

Obviously he cannot live in the house and also rent it because it is a single-family house.

> <u>OR</u> can also indicate three or more choices:

> For the same amount of money the Wheelers can spend two weeks in Europe, they can fly in their plane to several places in Mexico for three weeks, **OR** they can buy a small sailboat.

USING <u>NOR</u> AS A CONNECTOR

Sometimes a person has two choices, but the person prefers not to accept either choice. You can write two sentences, using *not* in both, to indicate what the person will not do. The following example explains that Susan has two choices—taking more classes and keeping her job—but she prefers not to choose either one:

> Susan Ikami does not plan to take more classes. She does not intend to keep her job.

You can connect the two sentences with <u>AND</u> because both are about Susan's choices:

> Susan Ikami does not plan to take more classes, **AND** she does not intend to keep her job.

Another connector you can use between the two sentences about Susan is <u>NOR</u>, which is actually a combination of *not* and <u>OR</u>. Because *not* is combined with <u>OR</u>, you can omit *not* from the second sentence. Notice that the order of words changes after <u>NOR</u>: the auxiliary verb *does* comes before the subject *she:*

> Susan Ikami does not plan to take more classes, **NOR** does she intend to keep her job.

Use a comma and <u>OR</u> or <u>NOR</u> between two or more independent clauses.

EXERCISE 11A

Read the following sets of sentences, and decide whether one adds information to another or whether the set offers a choice. Use <u>AND</u>, <u>OR</u>, or <u>NOR</u> and appropriate punctuation to combine the following sentences.

1. Desert snakes sleep under a rock during the hottest part of the day.
   They seek shelter in a cool cave.

2. Snakes cannot live in extreme cold.
   They cannot live in extreme heat.

3. Some snakes live on the ground.
   Others live in water and in trees.

4. Snakes have no ears.
   They do not have movable eyelids.

5. The jaws of snakes are loosely jointed.
   They are extremely flexible.

EXERCISE 11B

Write at least five sentences about a single topic in which you discuss choices you or someone else might have. Use the connectors <u>OR</u> and <u>NOR</u> between the independent clauses expressing the choices in two or three of the sentences.

Show these sentences to your instructor or tutor.

PAIRED CONNECTORS

You can also indicate choices by using the following paired connectors, called correlative conjunctions:

> either . . . or   neither . . . nor

The word pattern that follows the first connector in the pair must also follow the second connector. For example, if you use a noun following *either,* you must also use a noun following *or:*

> Peter will order **either** a *desk* **or** a *table* for his new office.

You cannot change the pattern after the second connector. The pattern must stay the same just as it does in music. The first phrase in writing or in music sets a theme or pattern that is parallel with and repeated in the following phrases. In the preceding example the phrase *either a desk* sets the pattern for *or a table,* which follows. Such parallelism makes the second phrase more easily understandable because it follows the same pattern as the preceding phrase. Parallelism adds to the cohesiveness of sentences or parts of sentences by continuing with a pattern already presented to the reader.

In the following example *either a desk* is not parallel with *or buy a table* because only the second phrase contains a verb—the verb *buy:*

> *Not:*   Peter will order **either** a *desk* **or** *buy a table* for his new office.

Phrases can be made parallel by moving the connector to a new position in the sentence. The phrases in the preceding example can be made parallel by placing *either* before *order:*

> Peter will **either** *order a desk* **or** *buy a table* for his new office.

Here are other examples of parallel word patterns joined by the paired connectors to indicate choices or alternatives:

> *Adjectives:*   Brenda is **neither** *satisfied* **nor** *pleased* with her new apartment.
> *Verbs:*   She *must* **either** *drive* to work **or** *take* a bus.
> *Phrases:*   She must decide to live **either** *in her own apartment* **or** *in a friend's house.*
> *Clauses:*   **Either** *she will stay in the apartment for a month,* **or** *she will move out immediately.*

Other paired connectors are *both . . . and* and *not only . . . but also.* These connectors also must have parallel constructions after them. They are different from the first two that indicate choice because they indicate addition, just like the word <u>AND</u>:

> **Both** *Brenda* **and** her *roommate* work for an advertising agency.
> **Not only** do they write copy for the ads, **but** they **also** help with the layouts.

Note the change of word order in the second example above. In the first independent clause, the auxiliary verb *do* follows *not only* and comes before the subject *they.* In the second independent clause the subject *they* comes between *but* and *also.*

In revising some sentences with faulty parallelism, you may have to add words as well as rearrange words. In the following example, *he raced* has been added to make the second half an independent clause that matches the first half of the sentence:

> *Not:* **Not only** did Victor race cars **but also** hydroplanes.
> *But:* **Not only** did Victor race cars, **but** he **also** raced hydroplanes.

Use a comma and the connector between two independent clauses. Use no comma between two phrases joined by a connector.

EXERCISE 11C

Some word patterns in each of the following sentences are not parallel. Revise the sentences by moving connectors or rewriting a part of the sentence to make the patterns parallel.

EXAMPLE: Not only did Sarah Nielsen design clothes but also jewelry.

> Sarah Nielsen designed **not only** *clothes* **but also** *jewelry.*
> *Or:* **Not only** *did Sarah Nielsen design clothes,* **but** *she* **also** *designed jewelry.*

1. Jack either arranges for our trip today, or I travel alone.

2. The superintendent wanted neither the increased staff nor would he accept the additional budget.

3. The new officers will either move the main office to Chicago or to Atlanta.

4. The old dishwasher needs both a new pump and replacing the silverware basket.

5. The people must either mail the tax returns by midnight, or they must pay a fine.

EXERCISE 11D

Combine the following pairs of sentences by inserting correlative conjunctions *either . . . or, neither . . . nor, both . . . and,* and *not only . . . but also.* You may omit words or add words. Be sure that the word pattern following one connector is parallel with the word pattern following the other.

EXAMPLE: Pablo will buy a horse.
            Pablo will buy a sports car.

            Pablo will buy **either** *a horse* **or** *a sports car.*
            Or: **Either** *Pablo will buy a horse,* **or** *he will buy a sports car.*

1. Jake is a karate expert.
   Jake is an excellent wrestler.

2. The principal does not want to attend the convention.
   The teachers do not want to attend the convention.

3. George will repair the tractor and plow the field.
   He will hire Tom to do the plowing.

4. Judy will not give Ben a job.
   Judy will not lend Ben any money.

5. The new senator has not kept his campaign promises.
   He has not introduced legislation to meet his constituents' needs.

6. Celia exhibited her strength of character during the recent crisis.
   She has been a source of encouragement for many of her co-workers.

ASSIGNMENT : Alternation

Write a paragraph in which you discuss alternatives open to someone planning a field
trip, selecting or training personnel, planning a career or new business, or any other
topic of your choice. Use the connectors you have studied in this lesson to show the
choices. Also include any other connectors you have studied in preceding lessons to
make your paragraph cohesive. Label the paragraph *Alternation,* and hand it in to your
instructor.

Lesson 12

Emphasis, Enumeration, Summation

In your writing you may at times emphasize a point or perhaps list a series of points; and when you end a paper, you summarize the points. In each case you are showing your readers the relationships of the ideas, and you make your writing cohesive by tying the points together with connectors and transitions.

The following list shows the last three groups of connectors you will study in this unit. They emphasize, enumerate, and summarize points in your paper:

	CONJUNCTIVE ADVERBS
Emphasis	indeed
	in fact
	certainly
	to be sure
Enumeration	first, second, third
	first, next, finally
	furthermore
Summation	finally
	in summary
	in conclusion
	therefore

EMPHASIS

When you are firmly convinced about an idea, you want your readers to accept what you say as the truth. When you present your idea in a sentence, you may give even more weight to your belief by emphasizing it in a second sentence as in the following example:

Single sentences:
The mayor is overstepping his authority by changing the city council's decision about zoning in the downtown section. He is acting like a dictator.

But you have to let your readers know you are emphasizing a point by using connectors such as indeed, in fact, and certainly, which function as transitions and tie the sentences together. In the following example the semicolon connects the two sentences, and indeed acts as a transition and provides the emphasis for the second idea. A comma follows indeed:

> *Combined:*
> The mayor is overstepping his authority by changing the city council's decision about zoning in the downtown section; **indeed (in fact),** he is acting like a dictator.

You can also provide transition between the two sentences by placing in fact within the second sentence. Notice that commas enclose the transitional expression:

> He is, **in fact,** acting like a dictator.

You can also use adverbs such as *really, actually, surely, obviously,* and others as modifiers within sentences for emphasis. Because these words modify a word within the sentence, no commas enclose them:

> The council members are **really** upset by his unexpected action. **Obviously** he is not working with the members. He must **surely** realize that he is making enemies.

EXERCISE 12A

Connect or combine the following sentences by using connectors such as indeed, in fact, certainly, and to be sure and adverbs such as *really, actually, surely,* and *obviously* to express emphasis. Use punctuation wherever it is needed.

1. The Harringtons neglect their children. The children always seem hungry and poorly clothed.

2. Since the accident Jim Stone seems out of touch with the world. He no longer knows the names of his wife and children.

3. Senator Miriam Glass has supported the senior citizens' project from the beginning. She has made personal contributions each year for at least five years.

4. Joe Feldon was badly hurt on the job last week. He will not be able to work for at least a month.

5. The church members frequently raise money for worthy causes. They will want to take part in collecting food for Thanksgiving baskets.

EXERCISE 12B

Write two sentences in which you use <u>indeed</u>, <u>in fact</u>, <u>certainly</u>, and <u>to be sure</u> as connectors or transitions to express emphasis. Or write sentences with *really, actually, certainly, surely,* and *obviously* as adverbs for emphasis.

1.

2.

Show these sentences to your instructor or tutor.

ENUMERATION

When you studied words to show a time sequence, you learned that you can use <u>first</u>, <u>second</u>, and <u>third</u>, or <u>first</u>, <u>next</u>, and <u>finally</u> to show the order in which events happened. You may use these same words and also <u>furthermore</u> or <u>most importantly</u> to make writing cohesive when you list points that may not follow a time sequence. The words may instead show order of importance or simply itemize the points, but they are acting again as links between sentences:

> *Single sentences:*
> The veterinarian discussed five main points for keeping a dog healthy.
> Dogs of all ages should have a balanced diet.
> They should have rabies and distemper shots at regular intervals.
> They need adequate exercise every day.
> They should be brushed and bathed regularly.
> They should be given love and attention.

> *Combined sentences:*
> The veterinarian discussed five main points for keeping a dog healthy: **first,** dogs of all ages should have a balanced diet; **second,** they should have rabies and distemper shots at regular intervals; **third,** they need adequate exercise every day; **AND, fourth,** they should be brushed and bathed regularly. **Most importantly,** they should be given love and attention.

If you expand the topic about the care of dogs into a paragraph, you can use the second, third, and fourth sentences above as level 2 ideas. Then you add level 3 ideas to support the level 2 ideas. The connectors tie all the sentences together. In addition, each connector—<u>first</u>, <u>second</u>, <u>third</u>, and <u>fourth</u>—introduces the discussion about one aspect of caring for a dog:

1   The veterinarian discussed five main points for keeping a dog healthy.

    2   **First,** dogs of all ages should have a balanced diet.

        3   They need about twice as much carbohydrate as protein.

        3   In addition, they need fat, minerals, and vitamins.

        3   Water should be available at all times, and milk may be offered with meals.

    2   **Second,** dogs should have rabies and distemper shots at regular intervals to protect them.

        3   Rabies vaccine should be administered generally at three-year intervals.

        3   Distemper vaccine should first be administered to a puppy at nine weeks and at 12 to 14 weeks and then at one- or two-year intervals in a booster injection.

    2   **Third,** dogs need adequate exercise every day.

        3   Those living in apartments need an opportunity to run free or take a walk with the owner.

        3   Dogs living in houses with yards probably get enough exercise if the yard is large, but they should walk outside the yard at least once a day if they are confined to small quarters.

    2   **Fourth,** dogs should be brushed and bathed regularly.

        3   Brushing the dog's coat keeps it shiny and free from burrs or tangles that develop.

        3   Regular bathing removes soil and freshens the dog's coat.

    2   **Most importantly,** dogs should be given love and attention.

    C   To keep a dog healthy owners should provide a balanced diet, immunization for rabies and distemper, adequate exercise, regular brushing and baths, and love and attention.

EXERCISE 12C

Write a series of sentences that enumerate points in a program or in a discussion. Use suitable connectors such as <u>first</u>, <u>second</u>, <u>third</u>, or <u>first</u>, <u>next</u>, <u>finally</u>, <u>furthermore</u>, or <u>most importantly</u>. Add punctuation wherever it is needed.

1.

2.

3.

4.

5.

Show these sentences to your instructor or tutor.

SUMMATION

To summarize a paragraph, you can restate the topic sentence in a different way in a
sentence at the end of the paragraph. In the paragraph about the care of dogs, the concluding sentence began with *To keep a dog healthy.* These words are a part of the
topic sentence, which also summarizes the paragraph. Using essentially the same words
takes your reader from the opening to the conclusion and ties the paragraph together
cohesively.

You can also use connectors such as finally, in summary, in conclusion, therefore,
and most importantly to introduce the summarizing statement. For example, the sentence in the paragraph about care of dogs beginning with Most importantly could also
have been used as the concluding sentence in the paragraph:

> *Summation:* **Most importantly,** the owners should give the dogs the attention and love
> they need and deserve.

In other cases you can use a summarizing word to introduce the final paragraph of a
long essay. However, you can lead your reader into your summary more smoothly and
obviously if you avoid using in conclusion and in summary:

> *Acceptable:* **In conclusion,** Myron White urged that training officers adopt programs
> that serve the greatest number of people. He noted, **furthermore,** that in-
> dividuals could receive special training later on for the specific skills their
> jobs might require. Providing the general training first will make everyone
> productive immediately.

> *Improved:* Myron White urged, **therefore,** that training officers . . .

EXERCISE 12D

Fill in the blanks in the following paragraphs with connectors that emphasize, enumerate, show result or alternation, and summarize. Add punctuation if it is needed after
the connector. Use the chart on pages 124–26 to help you recall the connectors you
need.

The new electric typewriter Mrs. Hart bought for her secretarial service caused her

problems immediately. (1) _____ the on-off switch did not work every

time. (2)_____ she could not turn the typewriter on,

(3)_____ she could not turn it off. (4)_____ the typewriter

ribbon became jammed in the cartridge and would not advance. She solved that problem by inserting a new ribbon. (5) _____ the typewriter moved up two lines instead of one when she pushed the carriage return key. (6) _____ she had to turn the platten back manually for single-spacing. (7) _____ she discovered that the letter *h* was broken; (8) _____ she could not type her last name or any word with *h* in it. That last problem was the worst one. (9) _____ she had never before bought such a poorly constructed piece of equipment. She decided, (10) _____ to put the typewriter back into the box and return it to the store.

ASSIGNMENT: Emphasis, Enumeration, Summation

Write a paragraph in which you discuss a number of problems, the points in a program or plan, or anything else that can be enumerated. Show emphasis by repeating an idea in a new sentence. Then summarize the entire paragraph in the final sentence. Use connectors that express emphasis, enumeration, and summation and any other connectors you need to tie the sentences together and make your writing cohesive. Use the list on the first page of this lesson, or refer to the chart of connectors on pages 124-26 to refresh your memory. Label the paragraph *Emphasis, Enumeration, Summation,* and hand it in to your instructor.

Lesson 13

Summary of Connectors

Now that you have completed the lessons in this second unit, you should feel more confident that you can write clear, easily understandable sentences in paragraphs and essays than before. Not only have you become aware of the relationships of ideas expressed in sentences, but you have learned to use three kinds of connectors—coordinating conjunctions, conjunctive adverbs, and subordinating conjunctions—to express these relationships. Thus you have learned to make your writing cohesive so that your readers can easily remember the points you have made.

In this lesson you have a summary of the connectors and the relationships they express and a summary of the punctuation used with the connectors. Exercises that follow these summaries give you the opportunity to use the connectors and punctuation again. By becoming thoroughly familiar with the information in this lesson, you will be able to use it as a quick reference as you continue to practice writing and revising.

CONNECTORS AND THE RELATIONSHIPS THEY EXPRESS

RELATIONSHIP EXPRESSED	LESSON	COORDINATING CONJUNCTION	CONJUNCTIVE ADVERB	SUBORDINATING CONJUNCTION
Addition	6	AND	furthermore in addition moreover also again besides too	
Time	7	AND (then)	then first, second, third first, next, finally next later still later finally	WHEN WHENEVER WHILE AS BEFORE SINCE AFTER

RELATIONSHIP EXPRESSED	LESSON	COORDINATING CONJUNCTION	CONJUNCTIVE ADVERB	SUBORDINATING CONJUNCTION
				AS LONG AS UNTIL NOW (THAT) ONCE AS SOON AS
Cause	8	FOR		BECAUSE SINCE
Result (effect)	8	AND (therefore)	consequently as a result thus therefore then hence	
Purpose	8			SO THAT IN ORDER THAT
Similarity	9		similarly likewise in the same way also too	AS AS . . . AS
Contrast	9	BUT AND	on the one hand on the other hand nevertheless however on the contrary instead in comparison	THAN
Concession	10	YET BUT	nevertheless however admittedly to be sure	ALTHOUGH THOUGH EVEN THOUGH WHILE WHEREAS
Manner	10			AS AS IF AS THOUGH
Condition	10			IF PROVIDED THAT UNLESS
Alternation	11	OR NOR		
Emphasis	12		indeed in fact certainly to be sure	

RELATIONSHIP EXPRESSED	LESSON	COORDINATING CONJUNCTION	CONJUNCTIVE ADVERB	SUBORDINATING CONJUNCTION
Enumeration	12		first, second, third first, next, finally furthermore	
Summation	12		finally in summary in conclusion therefore	

PUNCTUATION WITH CONNECTORS

The following rules summarize the use of punctuation with the three kinds of connectors. Each of these rules has been explained in Lesson 6 to 12. Use this list mainly for reference.

Punctuation with Two or More Independent Clauses

In a sentence made up of two independent clauses, place a comma at the end of the first independent clause, then the coordinating conjunction [(, AND) (, BUT) (, OR)] followed by the second independent clause:

> Jed cleared the land in the forest, **AND** his son Tyler brought building materials for the cabin.

In a series of three or more independent clauses, a comma follows each independent clause. The coordinating conjunction comes before the last independent clause in the series:

> The two men laid the foundation, they connected pipes for water, **BUT** they had no source of electricity.

If either independent clause contains commas within it, use a semicolon (;) at the end of the first independent clause, then the coordinating conjunction:

> Elissa, Jed's daughter, found plans for installing solar panels for solar energy; **AND** Mary, his wife, bought wood-burning stoves for heating and cooking.

If no coordinating conjunction is used to combine two or more independent clauses, use a semicolon alone after each one:

> Each member of the family shared in building the cabin; they enjoyed the closeness the project made them feel.

If you use only a comma instead of a semicolon, you have a comma splice, indicated with the correction symbol *CS:*

Not: Each member of the family shared in building the cabin, they enjoyed the close-ness the project made them feel.

If you do not use punctuation and connectors between independent clauses, you have a run-on sentence, indicated by *Run-on:*

Not: Each member of the family shared in building the cabin they enjoyed the close-ness the project made them feel.

When a conjunctive adverb (however, in addition, nevertheless) is used between two independent clauses, place a semicolon at the end of the first independent clause, then the conjunctive adverb, followed in most cases by a comma:

They finally completed the cabin; **however,** not everything had gone smoothly.

If the conjunctive adverb appears within an independent clause, place commas before and after the conjunctive adverb:

They decided, **as a result,** not to do any more building.

Use a colon (:) or a dash (—) at the end of an independent clause to introduce an explanation or a series:

Jed had learned something about himself from the experience: he had strengthened ties with his family more than ever before; he could actually complete a project; he would never attempt to build a house in the city.

Punctuation with One Independent Clause and One or More Dependent Clauses

When the dependent clause appears at the beginning of the sentence, place a comma after it:

WHILE Tyler and Elissa sat outside the cabin, they decided to study architecture.

When the dependent clause interrupts an independent clause and appears within the independent clause, place a comma before and a comma after the dependent clause:

They decided, **AFTER** they had talked with their parents, to change their courses of study.

When the dependent clause appears at the end of the independent clause, use no comma:

Jed and Mary were pleased **BECAUSE** their son and daughter finally had goals.

EXERCISE 13

Read all of the following sentences, which make up a story. Then connect and combine the sentences, using the connectors you have studied, to show the relationship of ideas. Add punctuation wherever it is needed.

1. Dick Sanders planned to take his driver's test on Thursday.
   He had the time.

2. He was prepared for the test.
   He was not prepared for all that happened that day.

3. He left his driveway.
   He noticed that the left rear wheel made a thumping sound for about five minutes.
   He had turned the corner into the main thoroughfare.
   He heard nothing more.

4. At the Department of Motor Vehicles office he passed the written test easily.
   He and the driving examiner got into Dick's car.
   Dick headed slowly toward the street exit.

5. Dick approached the exit.
   Another driver turned his car suddenly into the exit.
   The other driver cut in front of Dick's car.

6. Dick slammed on the brakes immediately.
   His bumper scraped the right rear fender of the other car.

7. The other driver did not stop.
   He raced across the parking lot.
   He parked near the entrance to the building.

8. The examiner shook his head in disbelief.
   He told Dick to turn right into the street.

9. Dick was still upset.
   He waited to make a left turn.

10. The examiner repeated his instructions.
    Dick turned right.
    He headed toward the intersection at the end of the block at about 30 miles per hour.

11. He approached the intersection.
    He put on his brakes.
    The car would not stop.

12. He grabbed the emergency brake.
    The car kept moving.
    He turned the wheels right into the curb.

13. Both he and the examiner were jolted.
    The car jumped the curb.
    It smashed into a fire hydrant.

14. The examiner held the top of his head and groaned.
    The fire hydrant snapped off.
    A large column of water shot into the air.

15. People helped Dick and the examiner out of the car.
    The left tire burst.
    The car tilted left on its wheel rim.

16. Dick stood on the sidewalk, staring at his car and shaking his head.
    The examiner put his arm around Dick's shoulders.
    He suggested trying the test another day.

ASSIGNMENT: Connectors and Punctuation

Write a paragraph of at least ten sentences about a topic that interests you, or check out possibilities with your instructor or in the library. As you revise the paragraph, add connectors to make the relationship of ideas clear. Finally, add punctuation wherever it is needed. The final draft should contain eight to ten sentences. Label the paragraph *Connectors and Punctuation,* and hand it in to your instructor.

Unit 2

Review

The three kinds of connectors you studied in Unit 2 allow you to connect and combine sentences and show the relationship of ideas among these sentences. By using these connectors you can make your writing cohesive and add variety to your writing style.

The exercises in this review give you the opportunity to use the techniques you learned in both Units 1 and 2 to make your writing cohesive.

I. Adding Connectors
(15 points—1 point each)   SCORE _____

Read all of the sentences in the following paragraph. Next, determine the relationship of ideas expressed in a sentence or between two sentences. Then write a connector in the blanks to show the relationship of ideas, and add punctuation if it is needed. You may use connectors that express any of the following relationships: addition, time, cause, result, purpose, similarity, contrast, concession, manner, condition, alternation, emphasis, enumeration, and summation.

People face a crisis (1) _____ they lose their job. (2) _____

they have been fired, they may first be surprised or shocked (3) _____

they did not expect the dismissal. (4) _____ they may become angry

(5) _____ they believe the employer had no cause to fire them.

(6) _____ the first shock has worn off, they may become very sad,

even depressed, (7) _____ they feel rejected. (8) _____

they may become depressed (9) _____ they have lost the security of a

regular income. (10) _____ they go from one employer to another to

look for another job, they may continue to feel rejected. They may

(11) _____ lose their self-confidence and wonder whether they can

actually qualify for another job. (12) _____ , on the other hand, the

people have been laid off because of a business slowdown, they probably are not sur-

prised; (13) _____ they also may feel anger and rejection

(14) _____ they have lost their financial security. (15) _____

these people finally find another job, they usually regain their confidence in them-

selves; but they may watch more closely for signs of a future loss of a job.

II. Combining Sentences
   (35 points)   SCORE _____

The following paragraph contains short sentences with repeated terms and no connectors to show the relationship of ideas. Connect and combine the sentences, using
the techniques you learned in both Units 1 and 2. After you have read all the sentences,
place X before each sentence that can be a base sentence. Then draw a line through
unnecessary words, and insert the remaining words in the base sentences or connect
them with the base sentences. Add punctuation wherever it is needed. Your sentences
are evaluated as follows:

Connecting and combining	Plus 35 points _____
Fragment, run-on, comma splice	Minus 4 each _____
Misused connector, semicolon, or comma	Minus 3 each _____
Awkward wording, PA Agr, Ref, SV Agr, DM, MM,	
Shift, Tense (Checklist, inside back cover)	Minus 2 each _____
Spelling, comma omitted, capitalization	Minus 1 each _____

Bats are engaged in a battle for survival.

Moths are engaged in a battle for survival.

Bats need moths for food.

Moths do not want to be eaten.

Bats and moths each use their own kind of radar to find each other.

The bats use their signals to locate moths to eat.

The moths send out signals to keep from being eaten.

Bats fly.

Bats send out high-pitched sounds above the range that people can hear.

The sounds hit the moth.

The sounds echo back to the bat's brain.

One sound is a steady tone.

The sound allows the bat to estimate the speed of its prey.

The sound allows the bat to estimate the direction of the prey's flight.

Another kind of sound accurately locates the target.

The bats are not always successful in capturing moths.

The moths send out a signal similar to the sound the bats make.

The bats often miss their targets.

III. Writing Sentences with Connectors
(50 points—5 points each)   SCORE _____

Write ten sentences in which you use one of the connectors listed after each number to connect or combine related ideas. You may use the connectors in any order you choose as long as you use one from each group.

1. AND, furthermore, in addition, moreover, also, besides
2. then, next, (first, second, third), WHEN, WHILE, AS, BEFORE, SINCE, AFTER
3. BECAUSE, SINCE, FOR
4. consequently, as a result, therefore, then
5. BUT, on the one hand, on the other hand, nevertheless, however, THAN
6. YET, ALTHOUGH, EVEN THOUGH, WHILE
7. AS, AS IF, AS THOUGH
8. IF, UNLESS, PROVIDED THAT
9. OR, NOR
10. finally, in summary, therefore

Your sentences are evaluated as follows:

Content	25 points _____
Form	25 points _____
	Total _____
Fragment, run-on, comma splice	Minus 5 _____
Misused connector, semicolon, comma	Minus 4 _____
Awkward wording, PA Agr, Ref, SV Agr, DM, MM, Shift,	
Tense (Checklist, inside back cover)	Minus 3 _____
Spelling, comma omitted, capitalization	Minus 1 _____
	Total _____
	TOTAL _____

1.

2.

3.

4.

5.

6.

7.

8.

9.

10.

Show this Unit Review to your instructor or tutor.

Combining Sentences by Embedding

If you have ever spent time walking through the streets of a city or town, going into the buildings and houses, and talking with the residents, you soon become thoroughly acquainted; and you may feel very much at home. When you leave the city, you might look back over it from a hill or from a plane and see how all the streets, buildings, and people fit comfortably together to make the city or town a place you enjoy visiting.

You can also gain a perspective of what you have learned by looking back briefly at lessons you have studied in detail. Such an overview helps you see how the details fit together to form a pattern that you can understand and apply to further study. It seems appropriate, therefore, to outline briefly what you have learned in the first two units of this text because the concepts are a foundation for what you will learn in the remaining units.

In Unit 1 you learned techniques to make your writing cohesive such as general/specific-term relationships, repetition of terms, modification, reference, consistent point of view, and meaning in single sentences. Then in Unit 2 you learned to connect and combine two or more related sentences, using coordinating conjunctions and conjunctive adverbs between independent clauses to show that two ideas receive equal emphasis:

> The number of people over age 55 is growing at twice the rate of the general population, **AND** these people make up 20 percent of the population.

You also learned to combine an independent clause with a dependent adverbial clause, using a subordinating conjunction as the connector to show that an idea supports or elaborates on a main idea:

AFTER their children have grown and left home, many senior citizens have money to spend for luxuries such as meals in restaurants, entertainment, and travel.

In Unit 3 you will study two more kinds of dependent clauses—the adjective clause and the noun clause. Like dependent adverbial clauses, adjective clauses and noun clauses allow you to show that one idea is subordinate to the idea in the main clause because they are embedded or inserted in the independent clause:

Businesses **THAT want to attract senior citizens as customers** are offering new products made especially for this group of people.

WHETHER the senior citizens will actually buy the new products is still uncertain.

Using the techniques you are learning to make your writing cohesive will help you write well-constructed, informative papers that readers will find helpful and enjoyable to read.

Lesson 14

Adjective Clauses

You built a foundation for your understanding of adjective clauses, a second kind of dependent clause, in Lessons 1, 3, and 5. Exactly how all the information fits together will become clear as you progress through this lesson, but the following brief review serves as a reminder of the points you learned. In Lesson 1, for example, you learned to identify general and specific terms: *building/Sears Tower, woman/daughter/Linda.* Then in Lesson 3 you placed adjectives before and after general terms to make them specific: *Bengal tiger; small cubs, soft and cuddly.*

When you studied pronouns in Lesson 5, you learned that the personal pronouns *he, she, it,* and *they* can take the place of nouns in other sentences. Because these pronouns refer to the nouns, the nouns and pronouns establish a relationship and a connection between and among sentences and make writing cohesive. In the following example *decision* appears in both the first and second sentences:

> *Original:* Darrell made a **decision**. The **decision** changed his life.

To eliminate the unnecessary repetition of *decision,* you can use the pronoun *it* in the second sentence. *It* refers to *decision:*

> *Revised:* Darrell made a **decision**. **It** changed his life.

In the next example *friends* appears in both sentences:

> *Original:* Darrell left some **friends**. He had known the **friends** for several years.

The plural noun *friends* can be replaced in the second sentence with *them:*

> *Revised:* Darrell left some **friends**. He had known **them** for several years.

All of the preceding information applies to adjective clauses, sometimes called relative clauses, because they function just like single-word adjective modifiers and they are related to the independent clause by pronoun reference. First, you will study the relative pronouns that link the adjective clauses to the base sentence, and then you will practice using adjective clauses as modifiers.

RELATIVE PRONOUNS

Relative pronouns take the place of the nouns they refer to just as personal pronouns do, but relative pronouns function differently from personal pronouns. Relative pronouns introduce adjective clauses, which are embedded or placed within base sentences. The relative pronouns that serve as connectors are the following:

> *who/whom/whose* refers to people
> *which* refers to objects or ideas
> *that* refers to people, objects, or ideas

Using the two sentences about Darrell, you can combine them in the following way:

Use *that* in place of *it* to refer to *decision.* Place the adjective clause beginning with *that* immediately after *decision,* the noun it modifies:

> Darrell made a **decision.** ~~It~~ changed his life.
> Darrell made a **decision** **that** changed his life.

Use *whom* in place of *them* to refer to *friends:*

> Darrell left some **friends.** He had known ~~them~~ for several years.
> Darrell left some **friends** **whom** he had known for several years.

That changed his life and *whom he had known for several years* are not independent clauses because they cannot stand alone as sentences; they are fragments. They function as adjectives by telling *which one:*

> Darrell made a **decision.** Which one? . . . (the one) **THAT** changed his life.
> Darrell left some **friends.** Which ones? . . . (the ones) **WHOM** he had known for several years.

Who/whom/whose

When *who* functions as a relative pronoun, it may introduce an adjective clause that makes a general term specific:

> Darrell did not want to leave a **friend WHO** had listened patiently to all his troubles. (Which friend?)

Who may also introduce an adjective clause that gives extra information about a specific term such as *Donna:*

> Darrell did not want to leave **Donna, WHO** had listened patiently to all his troubles.

Who has three forms: *who,* used as a subject; *whom,* used as an object; and *whose,* used as an adjective within the clause. To decide whether to use *who* or *whom,* substitute *he, she,* or *they* for *who* and *him, her,* or *them* for *whom:*

> **she** had listened . . .
> Darrell did not want to leave Donna, **WHO** had listened patiently to all his troubles.

> He had met **her** . . .
> Darrell liked Donna, **WHOM** he had met on the job.

Whose is the possessive form, used to show ownership. In the following example *whose* refers to *Donna:*

> He valued **her** opinions.
> Darrell trusted Donna, **WHOSE** opinions he valued.

That

When *that* functions as a relative pronoun, it introduces an adjective clause that makes a general term specific. In the following example *advice* is a general term. *That his friends gave him* is an adjective clause that modifies *advice* and makes *advice* specific. If the adjective clause were deleted, readers would ask which advice Darrell decided not to take:

> Darrell decided not to take the **advice.**   Which advice?
> Darrell decided not to take the **advice THAT** his friends gave him.

Sometimes the word *that* is not stated, but the relationship of the two parts stays the same:

> Darrell decided not to take the **advice (THAT)** his friends gave him.

Which

When *which* functions as a relative pronoun, it usually introduces an adjective clause that gives extra information about a specific term. In the following example, *his car* is a specific car. The adjective clause *which he had owned for ten years* gives extra information about Darrell's car. If the adjective clause is deleted, the base sentence still gives full information about Darrell's activities:

> Early one morning Darrell packed his belongings into his car.
> Early one morning Darrell packed his belongings into **his car, WHICH** he had owned for ten years.

Sometimes *which* functions like *that* to introduce an adjective clause that makes a general term specific; however, many writers prefer using *that:*

> Darrell decided not to take the **advice WHICH** his friends gave him.

Note: You may have noticed that a comma appears before the adjective clause in some of the preceding examples and not in others. The use of commas with adjective clauses will be explained on pages 143–44.

EXERCISE 14A

To help you understand the process for combining sentences by making one an adjective clause, you should work with each set of sentences given below in four steps:

1. Read the set of sentences, and underline the noun that is repeated in each sentence:

> Dan bought a car.
> The car gave him trouble from the start.

2. Substitute a personal pronoun *(he/him, she/her, it, they/them)* in one of the sentences for the repeated noun:

> Dan bought a car.
> It gave him trouble from the start.

3. Identify the base sentence by placing X before it. Substitute a relative pronoun *(who/whom/whose, which,* or *that)* for the personal pronoun to change the sentence to an adjective clause:

> X   Dan bought a car.
>
> **THAT**
> It̶   gave him trouble from the start.

4. Place the adjective clause immediately after the noun that it modifies in the independent clause when you combine the sentences:

> *Independent clause Adjective clause - - - - - - - - - - - - - - - - -*
> Dan bought a car   **THAT** gave him trouble from the start.

Note: Do not add punctuation to any of the following sentences because it is not needed.

1.   The woman called the police.

   The woman's house had been burglarized.

2.   People seem to enjoy the novel.

   The novel concentrates on the author's childhood during the depression in the 1930s.

3. American customs sometimes seem peculiar to refugees.

   Refugees come to the United States from Indochina.

4. Karen hired artists' models.

   She used the artists' models in the life drawing class at the art school.

5. During the Middle Ages in Europe kings and knights lived in castles.

   The castles were destroyed and rebuilt several times in later years.

6. In the Dallas area visitors can see man-made lakes.

   The man-made lakes serve as water sources and recreational areas.

CHOOSING THE BASE SENTENCE

In the last exercise the first sentence in each set was the base sentence, and the second sentence became the adjective clause. However, if both sentences in a set give information of the same importance, either sentence can become the base sentence. The sentence you choose to be the base sentence is the one you want to emphasize in relation to the other sentence. In the following example either sentence can become the base sentence by using *that* in place of *the house:*

X The house / needs paint.	**/THAT/** ~~The house~~ needs paint.
/THAT/ Jack owns ~~the house~~.	X Jack owns the house / .
The house **THAT Jack owns** needs paint.	Jack owns the house **THAT needs paint.**

Notice that the adjective clause comes immediately after *the house,* the noun that it modifies, in both combined sentences. In the example on the left above, *that Jack owns* is inserted into the sentence between the subject and verb. In the example on the right above *that needs paint* appears at the end of the sentence.

In some cases only one of the sentences in the set can be the adjective clause. In the following example the second sentence shows the result of committing crimes; therefore, it should be the base sentence. The sentence marked *Not* may be a possible combination, but not a usual one:

People commit crimes.
X People receive penalties.

People **WHO commit crimes** receive penalties.
Not: People who receive penalties commit crimes.

In the next set the second sentence becomes the base sentence because people usually do not develop computer programs unless they have a computer to work with:

People buy home computers.
X People sometimes develop programs for their own use.

People **WHO buy home computers** sometimes develop programs for their own use.

In the last set *woman* and *property* appear in each sentence; as a result, a relative pronoun can replace either word in a combined sentence. Here are the possibilities, which are limited because of the time sequence:

The woman bought the property.
X The woman sold the property the next week.

X The woman bought the property.
The woman sold the property the next week.

The woman **WHO bought the property** sold it the next week.

The woman bought the property **THAT she sold the next week.**

With a slight change of words, word order, and verb tense you can produce the following sentences:

The woman **WHO sold the property** had bought it the week before.
The next week the woman sold the property **THAT she had bought.**

EXERCISE 14B

Read both sentences in the following sets. Next, place X before the sentence you believe should be the base sentence. Then combine the sentences, making one an adjective clause that modifies a noun in the base sentence.

EXAMPLE: X Mary owns a black horse.
The black horse injured its leg.

Mary owns a black horse.
X The black horse injured its leg.

Mary owns a black horse **THAT injured its leg.**

The black horse **THAT Mary owns** injured its leg.

1. About one thousand people boarded the cruise ship.
The cruise ship sailed through the inland passage to Alaska.

2. The rooster crowed every morning.
   The rooster woke the neighbors.

3. In early spring birds landed in the back yard.
   Birds had migrated north.

4. The children built a treehouse.
   The treehouse had three rooms.

5. The sailors painted the hull of the oil tanker.
   The sailors were on duty.

6. The young man had bought a new car.
   The young man wrecked the new car a month later.

PUNCTUATION WITH ADJECTIVE CLAUSES

You learned that *that* introduces adjective clauses that make general terms specific
and *which* usually introduces adjective clauses that give extra information about
specific terms. You also learned that *who* may introduce adjective clauses that make
general terms specific or that add information to specific terms. The following examples show when to use commas with adjective clauses.

    No commas are used when the adjective clause makes a general term specific. In
the following example the adjective clause beginning with *that Bruce Ito had prepared . . .* makes *plan* in the base sentence specific because it tells *which plan:*

> The executive committee discussed the plan **THAT Bruce Ito had prepared for
> reorganizing the sales staff.**

Commas enclose (appear before and after) an adjective clause that gives extra information about a specific term such as *Bruce Ito* in the next example:

> Bruce Ito, **WHO heads a management consulting firm,** had prepared a comprehensive,
> twenty-page report.

An adjective clause may give extra information about a general term that has already been identified in a preceding sentence. In the following example, readers recognize that *the certificate* in the second sentence refers to *Achievement Award Certificate* in the first sentence; therefore, the adjective clause following it is enclosed in commas:

> Jane was pleased to receive the Achievement Award Certificate, **WHICH gave her recognition for her outstanding work the past two years.** The glass covering the framed certificate, **WHICH she dropped accidentally,** broke into tiny pieces.

EXERCISE 14C

Combine the following sentences by changing one sentence to an adjective clause. First, place X before the base sentence. Then use a relative pronoun *(who/whom/ whose, which,* or *that)* in place of the repeated noun. Then enclose in commas only those adjective clauses that give extra information about a specific noun.

1. Mitzi works for a considerate employer.
   The employer provides excellent working conditions.

2. Mitzi earns extra money.
   The extra money covers unexpected expenses.

3. Some years the employer gives her a generous bonus.
   She uses the bonus for travel with her husband and children.

4. Every year Mitzi plants a huge vegetable garden.
   She takes care of the garden in her spare time.

5. Mitzi sells most of the vegetables.
   She raises the vegetables.

6. The extra income enables her to enjoy luxuries.
   She could not afford the luxuries otherwise.

7. Her husband seldom helps her with the garden.
   Her husband spends long hours traveling and seeing customers.

8. Mitzi's eight- and ten-year-old daughters seem to enjoy the garden.
   The daughters help their mother.

POSITION OF ADJECTIVE CLAUSES

To keep the meaning of the sentence clear, place each adjective clause as close as possible to the noun it modifies. If you change the second sentence in the following set to an adjective clause, you must insert it immediately after *Mr. Wilson,* the noun that it modifies, to keep the reference clear:

>   X Mr. Wilson **/** listens closely to the young men.
> **/, WHO/** ~~Mr. Wilson~~ wears a hearing aid. **/,/**

>   *Not:* Mr. Wilson listens closely to the young men **who wears a hearing aid.**
>   *But:* Mr. Wilson, **who wears a hearing aid,** listens closely to the young men.

Combining the next set of sentences appears simple. You can use *which* in place of *Ben's cabin in the El Dorado Forest* to change the first sentence to an adjective clause:

> **/, WHICH/** ~~Ben's cabin in the El Dorado Forest~~ burned last year. **/,/**
>   X Ben's cabin in the El Dorado Forest is a total loss.

However, inserting the adjective clause into the base sentence must be done with care. If you place *which burned last year* after *Forest,* the combined sentence seems to say that the Forest burned:

>   *Not:* Ben's cabin in the El Dorado Forest, **WHICH burned last year,** is a total loss.

You can place the adjective clause after *cabin,* or you can keep two sentences:

>   *But:* Ben's cabin, **WHICH burned last year in the El Dorado Forest,** is a total loss.
>   *Or:* Ben's cabin in the El Dorado Forest burned last year. The **cabin** is a total loss.

You can see from the examples above that you must clearly understand the sentences in a set and then keep the meaning in mind as you combine two or more sentences. Sometimes two simple sentences explain ideas more clearly than a combined sentence when the reference is unclear.

FAULTY PRONOUN REFERENCE

You will find that some writers use *which* to refer to a whole idea rather than just one noun as in the sentence that follows:

> Kevin did not come home last night, **WHICH worried his parents.**

Such a sentence is not clearly written because the relationship of ideas is suggested rather than explicit. The weakness lies in the clause *which worried his parents* because it does not answer *which one,* and there is no noun in the sentence for it to modify. You can examine the relationship of ideas in the two parts of the sentence by changing the adjective clause to a question:

> Kevin did not come home last night. Why were his parents worried?

The sentence about Kevin gives a cause, and the question indicates a result (or effect)—Kevin's parents worried. This relationship can be shown by using the subordinating conjunction *because* to combine the sentences:

> Kevin's parents worried **BECAUSE he did not come home last night.**

EXERCISE 14D

In the following sentences the adjective clause may be misplaced or the relative pronoun may not have a noun to refer to. First, underline the adjective clause. Then write the two parts of the sentence as separate sentences, or you may want to write the adjective clause as a question first, using *who, what,* or *why* in place of *which.*

EXAMPLE: The sales representative received a large order for stationery, <u>which surprised him</u>.

> *Two sentences:* The sales representative received a large order for stationery. What surprised him? The size of the order.

> *Revised:* The sales representative received a large order for stationery. The size of the order surprised him.

> *Or:* The sales representative was surprised because he received a large order for stationery.

EXAMPLE: The flowers bloomed early in the spring <u>that Hazel had planted in the fall</u>.

> *Two sentences:* The flowers bloomed early in the spring. Hazel had planted them in the fall.

> *Revised:* The flowers **that Hazel had planted in the fall** bloomed early in the spring.

1. Joe plans to visit San Francisco for a week, which pleases Scott.

2. The promotion came after many years, which she had earned.

3. Marsha disliked everybody, which Nelson could not stand.

4. Candy lost the suitcase last week that she had packed with dirty clothes.

5. The new car cost much more than Carlos had expected, which disappointed him.

6. The newspaper lay on the coffee table that contained depressing reports.

EXERCISE 14E

Combine the following sets of sentences by completing these steps. First, read the sentences in a set, and decide what the relationship of ideas is. Is one sentence showing an alternative idea, a result, a time relationship? Or does it offer additional information about a noun in one of the other sentences? After you answer the question, place X before the base sentence. Then write the connector you intend to use before the sentence that you will change to a dependent clause. Refer to the list of connectors in Lesson 13, and also consider using the relative pronouns *who/whom, which,* and *that.* Next, indicate the punctuation, if any, before and after the clause. Finally, combine the sentences.

EXAMPLE: */, WHO/* ~~Steve and Karen Olsen~~ enjoy traveling. */,/*
            X   Steve and Karen Olsen sometimes spend their vacation in the
                United States.

            Steve and Karen Olsen, **WHO enjoy traveling,** sometimes spend their
            vacation in the United States.

X   They take hundreds of photographs.
/BECAUSE/   They want to remember all the places of interest.

They take hundreds of photographs **BECAUSE** they want to remember all the places of interest.

1.   Karen and Steve thoroughly enjoyed a recent seven-day trip.
        They took a seven-day trip through the New England states.

2.   In each of the states they visited historical sites.
        They had read about historical sites in novels and history books.

3.   In Plymouth, Massachusetts, for example, they boarded a replica of the *Mayflower.*
        The replica of the *Mayflower* had been built in England and sailed across the Atlantic in 1957.

4.   Karen and Steve stood on the deck of *Mayflower II.*
        Karen and Steve tried to imagine the experiences.
        The 102 Pilgrims had had experiences sailing across the Atlantic for sixty-six days in 1620.

5.   In Plymouth, Vermont, they went through President Calvin Coolidge's home.
        They had visited his birthplace just across the road.

6.   Once again Steve and Karen put their imaginations to work.
        Steve and Karen thought about the night.
        That night Vice-President Calvin Coolidge heard in his home about the death of President Warren G. Harding in San Francisco.

7.   Coolidge's father, a judge, almost immediately administered the oath
             of office of President of the United States to Calvin Coolidge.
             Calvin Coolidge became the thirtieth president.

EXERCISE 14F

Write five sentences with adjective clauses. Use the relative pronoun given after each
number to introduce the adjective clause.

1. (WHO)

2. (WHOM)

3. (WHICH)

4. (THAT)

5. (WHOSE)

Show these sentences to your instructor or tutor.

ASSIGNMENT: Adjective Clauses

Write a paragraph of eight to ten sentences. Include at least three sentences or more
in which you use relative pronouns to combine related ideas. As you have learned in
this lesson, you need repeated terms in sentences so that you can use a relative pronoun in place of a noun in one of the sentences. Choose a topic, then, that allows you
to repeat terms. When you write about people and their activities, for example, you can
use *who/whom/whose* to refer to them. If you write about business, a job, or a game,
you probably can use *which* or *that.* Revise your paragraph as many times as necessary
to show the proper relationship of ideas among your sentences. Label the paragraph
Adjective Clauses, and hand it in to your instructor.

Lesson 15

Noun Clauses

You probably have written sentences similar to the following one:

> The pilot thought **she would be ready to take off at 10 a.m.,** but then she discovered **THAT her passenger was delayed in traffic.**

However, you may not have been aware that you had combined several sentences:

	The pilot thought ~~something~~.	
/(THAT)/	She would be ready to take off at 10 a.m.	**/,/**
/BUT/	Then she discovered ~~something~~.	
/THAT/	Her passenger was delayed in traffic.	

In the example above, *something* in the first and third sentences is a vague, general word. After you delete it from the first sentence, you substitute specific information—*she would be ready to take off at 10 a.m.*—and connect it with THAT (or THAT understood). You combine the third and fourth sentences in the same way. By eliminating vague words such as *something, this, that,* and *it,* you save your readers the task of guessing what the vague word stands for. In addition, you make your writing cohesive because you relate the ideas closely to one another.

When you use *she would be ready to take off at 10 a.m.* in place of *something,* the word group then functions as a noun clause, the third kind of dependent clause. A noun clause may appear in a sentence where nouns usually appear. Noun clauses may begin with *who, whoever, which, what, whether, where, why, when,* and *how.* Here are examples with four of these introductory words:

> **WHAT Dino has said** should not disturb his friends because they know **WHY he is angry.**
> **WHETHER he eventually solves his problems** depends on **HOW cooperative his wife can be.**

Although noun clauses may look like adjective or adverbial clauses when they begin with such connectors as *who, that, when,* or *why,* they are **not** additions to sentences as adjective and adverbial clauses are. They are a *necessary part of the sentence* because they function in one of the noun positions in the basic sentence. As a result, **no**

commas enclose noun clauses. If you remove a noun clause from a sentence, you have only a part of a sentence left. For example, the noun clause in the first sentence below is necessary because it completes the verb. In the second sentence the noun clause functions as the subject of the verb *is:*

> Automobile drivers should be aware ~~THAT they have certain responsibilities.~~
> ~~WHAT they do at the time of an accident~~ is important.

Knowing how noun clauses fit into sentences will help you in revising and editing what you write. If you find that you have written a sentence beginning or ending with *something, this, that,* or *it,* which refers generally to a preceding idea rather than a particular noun, you might be able to substitute a noun clause for these general terms. Before you combine the sentences, draw a line through the word or words to be deleted:

/THAT/
> ~~Something~~ is certain now.
> Toni will become a physician.

> **THAT Toni will become a physician** is certain now.

/(THAT)/
> Toni believes ~~this~~.
> She will earn her doctor's degree next year.

> Toni believes **(THAT) she will earn her doctor's degree next year.**

/(THAT)/
> She knows ~~something~~.
> She has many more hours of hard work ahead of her.

> She knows **(THAT) she has many more hours of hard work ahead of her.**

Another way to use a noun clause is to combine a question with a statement by making the question a noun clause. In the following example, the question is rewritten as a statement, and it is introduced by WHETHER. The noun clause takes the place of *this* in the first sentence:

/WHETHER/
> The question is ~~this~~.
> Will Joel be able to afford the new car?

> The question is **WHETHER Joel will be able to afford the new car.**

Frequently the word beginning a question—WHO, WHICH, WHAT, WHERE, and others—can become the introductory word for a noun clause:

/WHERE/
> Where will Joel get the extra money?
> ~~It~~ is a problem he must solve.

> **WHERE Joel will get the extra money** is a problem he must solve.

To combine the next pair of sentences you can begin the noun clause with WHEN and omit *some time* in the second sentence:

                      Joel wonders ~~something~~.
    /WHEN/   Joel will get a pay raise ~~some time~~.

                      Joel wonders **WHEN he will get a pay raise.**

The phrase *in some way* in the second sentence below can be changed to HOW to
combine the two sentences:

                      Joel thought about ~~something~~.
    /HOW/   Joel could get a short-term loan ~~in some way~~.

                      Joel thought about **HOW he could get a short-term loan.**

EXERCISE 15A

For further practice in understanding noun clauses, combine the following pairs of
sentences by making one a noun clause that becomes a part of the other sentence.
First, place X before the base sentence. Next, cross out words to be deleted. Then
place an introductory word at the beginning of the noun clause. Finally, write the
combined sentence.

EXAMPLE: X Tina knew ~~this~~.
            /THAT/ Michael was having serious personal problems.

                    Tina knew **THAT Michael was having serious personal
                    problems.**

1.   X Hans decided something.
    /WHEN/   He would drive through France some time.

2.   X Sonia knows it.
    /THAT/   She will want a larger house soon.

3.   Why did Ted refuse the promotion?
                 That is a mystery.

4.   The scholarship committee knows something.
                 Who will receive the award?

5.   The well-trained athlete asked this.
                Did he qualify for the basketball team?

EXERCISE 15B

Write sentences with noun clauses. Use the words given in parentheses after each number to introduce the noun clause. To do this exercise in steps, you can first write two sentences or a sentence and a question. Then combine them into a single sentence.

EXAMPLE: X Jan does not know ~~something~~.
       /WHERE/ Where will he find paint to match the paint on his car?

                Jan does not know **WHERE he will find paint to match the paint on his car.**

1. (WHO or WHOEVER)

2. (WHETHER)

3. (WHEN)

4. (THAT)

5. (WHY)

Show these sentences to your instructor or tutor.

EXERCISE 15C

Take one of the paragraphs you wrote for Unit 2 or Unit 3 assignments, and find the noun clauses you have written in your paragraph. Underline them in the paragraph, and then show the sentences to your instructor or tutor.

ASSIGNMENT: Noun Clauses

Write a paragraph of about eight to ten sentences in which you express an opinion (think, know, believe) or explore the possibilities of something (wonder whether, how, why, etc.). Include at least three sentences with noun clauses. Label the paragraph *Noun Clauses,* and hand it in to your instructor.

Unit 3

Review

I. Combining Sentences
(48 points—3 points each)   SCORE _____

Combine the following sets of sentences by using the techniques you have learned in this text to connect and combine sentences and make writing cohesive. Use punctuation wherever it is needed.

1. A huge crowd of friends gathered at the Hot Rod Raceway.
   The friends had brought baskets of food and coolers with drinks.
   The Raceway was outside of town.
   They were attending the Junk-yard Car Race.
   The race was annual.

2. The contestants were ten men and four women.
   The ten men and four women had bought old cars for 100 dollars each.

3. The contestants could make no repairs.
   They could not change the cars in any way.

4. They were to drive as fast as they could.
   They were to drive as long as they could without stopping.

5. Mario drove a 1965 Ford.
   Mario was tall.
   Mario was slender.
   Mario sold life insurance.
   The Ford was blue.

6. Melissa had found a Chevrolet.
   Melissa was brown-eyed.
   Mario had encouraged Melissa to enter the race.
   The Chevrolet was bright red.

7. The race began on a clear morning.
   The morning was sunny.

8. John's car choked and sputtered noisily.
   John's car evidently had been in a wreck.

9. Shari led the rattling pack of junk cars.
   Shari could scarcely see above the steering wheel.
   Shari was petite.
   Shari was blonde.

10. The first hour Pete's car lost a wheel.
    Pete's car had no doors.
    The car lost the right wheel.

11. The second hour two cars became overheated and stopped.
    The two cars had been leading the pack.

12. At the end of the third hour Melissa was the only one on the track.
    Melissa felt her car stall for a minute.

13. The engine began missing.
    The engine was pounding.
    The muffler fell to the ground.
    The muffler was rusted.

14. The woman put on the brakes.
    The woman was exhausted.
    The woman was perspiring.
    The car kept rolling.

15. She shifted to low gear.
    She tried reverse.
    The car engine stalled.

16. Melissa climbed out.
    The crowd cheered loudly.
    The crowd was enthusiastic.
    Mario ran down the track.
    Mario ran to her.

II. Misplaced Modifiers and Faulty Pronoun Reference
    (12 points—3 points each)   SCORE _____

In the following sentences the adjective clause may be misplaced or the relative pronoun may not have a noun to refer to. If the modifier is misplaced, move it to the
word it modifies in the sentence. If pronoun reference is faulty, rewrite the sentence
to make the relationship of ideas logical.

1. Luggage manufacturers are adding wheels to various sizes of suitcases, which makes
   moving the heavy suitcases easy.

2. At the Alaska salmon bake, chefs coated pieces of fresh salmon with brown sugar and honey, which are caught off the coast of Alaska.

3. Marshall refused to be a witness against the accused burglar, which irritated the prosecutor.

4. Some motion pictures provide a glimpse of clothing styles, cars, and houses of earlier times, which were made in more recent times.

III. Writing Adjective Clauses
    (20 points—4 points each)   SCORE _____

Write five sentences with adjective clauses. Use the relative pronouns given after each number to introduce the adjective clause.

1. (WHO)

2. (WHOM)

3. (WHOSE)

4. (WHICH)

5. (THAT)

Show these sentences to your instructor or tutor.

IV. Writing Noun Clauses
    (20 points—4 points each)   SCORE _____

Write five sentences with noun clauses. Use the introductory words given after each number to introduce the noun clause.

1. (THAT)

2. (WHETHER)

3. (WHEN)

4. (WHY)

5. (WHO/WHOEVER)

Show these sentences to your instructor or tutor.

Combining Sentences by Deleting and Embedding

In the manufacture of a car engine, the designers create parts such as pistons, gears, and levers with characteristics that allow the parts to relate to and function with the other parts. People then assemble the manufactured parts and connect and combine them to make the engine. At this point the engine can run, but it usually does not operate smoothly. The third step is to refine its operation by tuning it so that it runs smoothly and efficiently.

In a similar manner the characteristics of the parts of a sentence allow them to function with other parts of the same sentence; the parts can also relate to the parts of other sentences. You studied these functions—making general terms specific, repeating terms, using pronouns in place of nouns, and sequencing verb tenses—in the first unit in this text, and you learned ways to use these functions to make your writing cohesive.

In Units 2 and 3 you learned to connect and combine sentences by using appropriate connectors. The connectors in some cases show that clauses in a sentence receive equal emphasis because they are coordinate (of equal rank). In other cases the connectors show that one or more clauses are subordinate (of lesser rank) in relation to an independent clause. In Unit 2 you combined sentences by connecting one clause to one or more other clauses. In Unit 3 you combined sentences by embedding (placing within) a clause in another clause. Your sentences became longer; however, your goal is not to write longer and longer sentences, especially if those sentences cause readers to lose their way before they get to the end. You are learning to use connectors to show the relationship of ideas and to make your writing cohesive.

In this unit you will continue to connect and embed clauses, but you will also learn to delete (omit) unnecessary words from a sentence and add the remaining words to another sentence or embed them within the sentence. The purpose is to develop flexibility in using a variety of ways to express your ideas and to make your writing clear, readable, and understandable for your readers.

Combining Coordinate Elements

In Lesson 3 you learned to combine sentences by first eliminating unnecessary words. Then you placed the remaining words before or after nouns in a base sentence to function as adjective modifiers. For example, each adjective printed in bold type in the second and third sentences below describes *stallion* in the first sentence:

SINGLE SENTENCES

Teresa rode the stallion along the beach.
~~The stallion was~~ **huge.**
~~The stallion was~~ **powerful.**

COMBINED SENTENCES

Teresa rode the **huge, powerful** stallion along the beach.
Or: Teresa rode the stallion, **huge** and **powerful,** along the beach.

In the preceding example the repeated words *The stallion was* in the sentences on the left are unnecessary and were, therefore, deleted. Then the adjectives *huge* and *powerful* were embedded in the first sentence before or after *stallion.*

The adjectives are coordinate (of equal rank) elements because you can use AND between them, and you can reverse their order: *huge and powerful* or *powerful and huge.* The comma replaces AND between the two adjectives.

In Lesson 6 you learned that you can make writing cohesive by using a comma and AND to express addition when you connect one sentence to another. You found that you can test this relationship of addition by including *also* in the second part of the combined sentences:

SINGLE SENTENCES

Justin Ellersbee served as the director of the art institute.
He taught art history there.

COMBINED SENTENCES

Justin Ellersbee served as the director of the art institute, **AND** he (also) taught art history there.

The two pieces of information about the art director receive equal emphasis because independent clauses have the same basic pattern: each has a subject-verb combination. In this case the subject-verb combinations are *Justin Ellersbee served . . .* and *he taught . . . .*

If the subject of the second sentence is the same as the subject of the first sentence, you can omit the second subject, but you do not change the emphasis. In the following example you increase the emphasis on the two positions Justin Ellersbee held. In other words, you lessen the emphasis on the subject, and you increase the emphasis on the predicate. Your decision about which way to write the sentence depends on how the sentence fits in with sentences before and after it in a paragraph and where you want to place the emphasis. The preceding version and the following one are both acceptable:

Justin Ellersbee served as the director of the art institute **AND** taught art history there.

Notice that you do not use a comma before <u>AND</u>. The reason is that you do not want to separate the second verb from its subject at the beginning of the sentence. The pattern looks like this: S V <u>AND</u> V. When, on the other hand, you connect two independent clauses, you separate them with a comma: S V, <u>AND</u> S V.

In this lesson you will learn to identify coordinate elements in sentences and embed them in a base sentence. With practice you will be able to delete unnecessary words to make your writing concise and thereby help your readers focus on the meaning of your sentence or paragraph.

COORDINATE ELEMENTS

In addition to adjectives and clauses, nouns, verbs, adverbs, or phrases may also be coordinate elements. In the following examples the unnecessary words have been crossed out because they repeat the same information monotonously without clarifying the meaning of the sentence. The remaining words and connectors have been inserted at the slash marks in the base sentences:

	SINGLE SENTENCES	COMBINED SENTENCES
Nouns:	**Teachers /** attended the conference. **Administrators** ~~attended the conference.~~	**Teachers AND administrators** attended the conference.
Verbs:	Jeff **jogged /** every day during the summer. ~~Jeff~~ **swam** ~~every day during the summer.~~	Jeff **jogged AND swam** every day during the summer.
Adverbs:	The professional speaker outlined the procedure **clearly /** . ~~The professional speaker outlined the procedure~~ **simply.**	The professional speaker outlined the procedure **clearly AND simply.**
Phrases:	The climbers hiked **over rocks /** . ~~The climbers hiked~~ **through forests.**	The climbers hiked **over rocks AND through forests.**

When you combine sentences with dependent clauses, you should repeat the subordinating conjunction or relative pronoun to indicate the beginning of each dependent clause:

Clauses:	Mark succeeded **because he paid**	Mark succeeded **because he paid**
	attention to detail / .	**attention to detail AND because**
	~~Mark succeeded~~ **because people**	**people cooperated with him.**
	cooperated with him.	

If sentences are in contrast with one another, you can use <u>BUT</u> or <u>YET</u> as the connector:

Susan **takes chances** / .	Susan **takes chances BUT observes**
~~Susan~~ **observes precautions.**	**precautions.**

When sentences indicate alternate choices, use <u>OR</u> or <u>NOR</u> as the connector:

Did Stan resign as president **because the**	Did Stan resign as president **because the**
members did not support his proposals?	**members did not support his proposals**
~~Did Stan resign as president~~ **because he has**	**OR because he has health problems?**
health problems?	

EXERCISE 16A

Combine the following sets of sentences. First, read all the sentences in a set. Next, choose one sentence to be the base sentence and place X before it. Third, draw a line through unnecessary words. Finally, place the remaining words in the base sentence, and use connectors where they are needed.

EXAMPLE: X The manufacturing company needed a new warehouse / .

/**AND**/ ~~The manufacturing company needed~~ a large garage.

The manufacturing company needed a new warehouse **AND** a large garage.

1. The owner asked several construction companies in the area for bids.
    The manager asked several construction companies in the area for bids.

2. The job included tearing down a building.
    The building was small.
    The building was vacant.
    The building was brick.
    The job included removing trees.
    There were two trees.
    The trees were diseased.
    The trees were elms.

3. The owner accepted the bid.
   The bid was the lowest.
   The manager set a date.
   It was for beginning construction.

4. The rumbling of the bulldozers gave the manager a headache.
   The banging of the bricks dropping in a dump truck gave the manager a headache.
   The headache was a throbbing one.
   The headache lasted for two days.

5. The noise of the building crews continued.
   The noise continued in the following weeks.
   The manager gradually paid less attention to it.

6. Soon the warehouse and garage were completed.
   The manager moved a desk into the new office.
   The manager moved file cabinets into the new office.
   The new office was in the warehouse.

7. The person in charge of repairs moved equipment.
   The equipment was for repairing trucks.
   The equipment was for repairing forklifts.
   The person moved the equipment into the garage.

8. The new work areas improved plant efficiency.
   The owner and the manager were pleased.

COORDINATE ELEMENTS IN A SERIES

As you reread a paragraph you have written, you may want to combine three or more sentences or parts of sentences to bring ideas into a close relationship by deleting unnecessary words. However, keep your writing from becoming monotonous by including dependent clauses to express relationships you studied in Units 2 and 3. Once again, whether you combine sentences or keep them separate depends on how they fit into your paragraph.

The steps you follow to combine three or more coordinate elements are the same as for combining two coordinate elements. You will, however, have to include punctuation to help readers separate the elements in a series. The following examples show coordinate elements in a series separated by commas. Remember that elements are coordinate (equal to one another) when they are all nouns or adjectives or phrases or clauses. You cannot consider, for example, a noun and a clause coordinate because a noun is a part of a clause just as *tires* and *car* are not coordinate because tires are a part of a car.

Items in a series are separated by commas. A comma appears before AND to indicate that the last item is separate from the one preceding it:

SINGLE SENTENCES	COMBINED SENTENCES
The wedding decorations consisted of **flowers / .** ~~The wedding decorations consisted of~~ **crepe paper bells.** ~~The wedding decorations consisted of~~ **ribbons.**	The wedding decorations consisted of **flowers, crepe paper bells, AND ribbons.**
The dance instructor **explained the benefits of aerobic dancing / .** ~~The dance instructor~~ **demonstrated each step.** ~~The dance instructor~~ **then danced with the music.**	The dance instructor **explained the benefits of aerobic dancing, demonstrated each step, AND then danced with the music.**
The ten-year-old dog had a litter of **/** puppies. ~~Some puppies were~~ **white.** ~~Some puppies were~~ **black.** ~~Some puppies were~~ **brown.**	The ten-year-old dog had a litter of **white, black, AND brown** puppies.
Joan demanded to know **who had authorized the audit of the financial records / .** ~~Joan demanded to know~~ **what parts would be examined.** ~~Joan demanded to know~~ **when the audit would take place.**	Joan demanded to know **who had authorized the audit of the financial records, what parts would be examined, AND when the audit would take place.**

You may use BUT in a series to show contrast:

The jacket has **a large fleece collar.** The jacket has **a hood.** The jacket has **no pockets.**	The jacket has **a large fleece collar AND a hood, BUT no pockets.**

In the preceding example the first two sentences tell what the jacket has; therefore, *collar* and *hood* are joined by AND. Because the third sentence tells what the jacket does not have—*no pockets*—this last item has been connected by BUT to show contrast.

The next set of sentences shows alternation or choices Melanie has. You can combine them by using OR as the connector:

Melanie can use the prize money **for new clothes.**
~~Melanie can use the prize money~~ **for a short trip somewhere.**
~~Melanie can use the prize money~~ **for guitar lessons.**

Melanie can use the prize money **for new clothes, for a short trip somewhere, OR for guitar lessons.**

You may sometimes write three or four sentences that you believe you can combine into a single sentence by making some of the words parts of a series, but you may be mistaken if you do not read your sentences carefully. In the following set of single sentences, you can see that Bertha sold three items, two kinds of dinnerware and one kind of flatware:

Bertha sold **plastic dinnerware.**
Bertha sold **china dinnerware.**
Bertha sold **stainless steel flatware.**

In combining the sentences in the example above, you can delete *dinnerware* in the second sentence and place AND between *plastic* and *china* to indicate the two kinds of dinnerware. Then you need another AND to connect *dinnerware* and *flatware.* You do not use commas because AND joins only two words in each case: *plastic and china* and *dinnerware and flatware:*

Not: Bertha sold **plastic, china dinnerware, AND** stainless steel **flatware.**
But: Bertha sold **plastic AND china dinnerware AND** stainless steel **flatware.**

If you want to combine the sentences as a series, you must repeat *dinnerware:*

Or: Bertha sold **plastic dinnerware, china dinnerware, AND** stainless steel **flatware.**

You can also connect three or more sentences, but you probably will not delete any words because each sentence retains all its parts when it becomes an independent clause. The following example shows four sentences combined in two ways. In the first combined sentence, the independent clauses are separated by commas, and AND appears before the last one. In the second combined sentence semicolons separate the sentences because AND does not appear before the last one:

Paul invited the guests.
Max prepared the meal.
Jill served the drinks.
Paul cleaned the kitchen afterwards.

Paul invited the guests, Max prepared the meal, Jill served the drinks, AND Paul cleaned the kitchen afterwards.
Or: **Paul invited the guests; Max prepared the meal; Jill served the drinks; Paul cleaned the kitchen afterwards.**

If commas appear within any independent clause in a series, the independent clauses must then be separated by semicolons to help readers see where each independent clause ends:

Jim, Jean, and Kathy could not attend the party; Eileen came and helped serve the food; **AND** Monica and Britt brought appetizers.

EXERCISE 16B

Combine the following sets of sentences. First, read all the sentences in a set. Next, choose one sentence to be the base sentence, and place X before it. Third, draw a line through unnecessary words. Finally, place the remaining words in the base sentence, and use connectors and punctuation where they are needed.

EXAMPLE: X   Teachers at the art institute taught classes / .   /,/
~~Teachers~~ produced pieces of art / .   /,/
/**AND**/   ~~Teachers~~ judged art exhibits.

Teachers at the art institute taught classes, produced pieces of art, **AND** judged art exhibits.

1. One instructor taught students to design jewelry.
   He taught students to make jewelry.
   He taught students to sell jewelry.

2. Another instructor taught life drawing.
   She conducted fashion seminars.
   She photographed students' art work.

3. "Tubs" Reilly made huge ceramic jars.
   He made huge ceramic bowls.
   He made slender vases.

4. People wondered whether he was called "Tubs" because he was a huge man.
   People wondered whether he was called "Tubs" because he made huge jars and bowls.

5. Students had opportunities to exhibit their art work in the gallery at the institute.
   Students had opportunities to sell their art work to commercial buyers.
   Students had opportunities to sell their art work to individuals.

6. Students attended the annual ball at the institute just before Christmas.
   Teachers attended the annual ball at the institute just before Christmas.
   Guests attended the annual ball at the institute just before Christmas.
   They spent the evening dancing.
   They ate the Christmas foods arranged on the long table.

7. All those attending wore costumes from various periods in history.
   All those attending wore masks.
   All those attending wore jewelry.

8. At midnight the director of the institute asked judges to examine the costumes.
   He asked judges to select three winners.
   He asked judges to award prizes.

SUBJECT-VERB AGREEMENT
WITH COORDINATE ELEMENTS

When you studied verb tenses in Lesson 5, you learned that verbs in the present tense
have two forms; one is the base, and the other is the base + *s*. The base is used with
plural nouns and pronouns and the pronoun *I*. The base + *s* is used with singular nouns
and pronouns.

    If two sentences written in the present tense are combined, the subject might
change from singular to plural. Then the form of the verb has to be changed to agree
with the new subject:

SINGLE SENTENCES	COMBINED SENTENCES
Present Tense:	
Martha **walks** three miles each day.	Martha and her husband **walk** three
Her husband **walks** three miles each day.	miles each day.

In the preceding example the subjects *Martha* and *husband* are both singular in the
single sentences; therefore, the verb *walks* in the present tense must end in the suffix
-s. In the combined sentence the subject *Martha and her husband* is plural; therefore,
the verb *walk* in the present tense does not end in *-s.*

In the present perfect tense **has** is used with singular subjects and **have** with plural subjects:

> **Present Perfect Tense:**
> Martha **has walked** three miles each day. Martha and her husband **have walked**
> Her husband **has walked** three miles each three miles each day.
> day.

When two nouns are joined by <u>AND</u>, they sometimes form a unit, which is considered to be singular. The present tense or present perfect tense verbs are, therefore, singular:

> Bread and butter **makes** a good snack for the little boy.
> Ham and eggs **is** Mel's idea of a satisfying breakfast.

If you write about ham and eggs as separate items, the subject is plural:

> Ham and eggs **have** both gone up in price.

When two or more singular subjects are joined by the connectors *or, nor, either . . . or,* or *neither . . . nor,* the verb is singular:

> Mike *or* Joe **wants** to borrow the blue jacket.
> *Neither* Mike *nor* Joe **has** money to buy a jacket.

When two subjects, one singular and the other plural, are joined by *either . . . or* or *neither . . . nor,* the verb agrees with the noun nearer to it:

> *Neither* Nancy *nor* her brothers **believe** the strange story.
> *Either* the brothers *or* Nancy **intends** to talk with the neighborhood gossip.

EXERCISE 16C

Connect or combine the following sentences. First, read all the sentences in a set. Next, cross out unnecessary words. Then examine the words you have left. In some cases you will simply link the two sentences with a connector, such as <u>AND</u>, <u>BUT</u>, or <u>OR</u>. In others you will combine sentences by placing words from the second sentence into the base sentence. If the subject of the new sentence becomes plural, change the verb to agree with the subject. If necessary, change other words in the sentence to plural forms.

EXAMPLE: Janet operates a secretarial service.
Bruce sells used cars.

Janet operates a secretarial service, **AND** Bruce sells used cars.

EXAMPLE: Janet is the parent of two children.
Bruce ~~is the parent of two children.~~

Janet and Bruce **are** the **parents** of two children.

1. One child is a girl.
   The other child is a boy.

2. The girl is four years old.
   The boy is two years old.

3. Christine likes to play in the swimming pool.
   Jason likes to play in the swimming pool.

4. Janet has taken swimming lessons at a local swimming school.
   Bruce has taken swimming lessons at a local swimming school.

5. Janet has studied water ballet.
   Bruce has played water polo.

6. Janet enjoys swimming in their pool at home.
   Bruce enjoys swimming in their pool at home.

7. Janet wants their children to learn to swim.
   Bruce wants their children to learn to swim.

8. The parents can teach the children themselves.
   They can take the children to a swimming school.

9. Bruce enrolls Jason in the swimming school.
   Bruce enrolls Christine in the swimming school.

10. Jason soon learns to float.
    Christine quickly learns to swim.

11. Later Jason swims to the instructor in the deep end of the pool.
    Christine hesitates to go into the deep end.

12. Bruce is pleased with the children's progress.
    Janet is pleased with the children's progress.

ASSIGNMENT: Coordinate Elements

Write a paragraph in which you have eight to ten sentences in the completed version. Choose a subject that will allow you to use connectors that show addition, contrast, or alternation. You might write about two or more people and their activities or interests. Or you might discuss two or more objects or ideas in some detail. Begin by writing down your ideas. Then go back and revise your paragraph to remove unnecessary words and to connect coordinate elements. After you have completed that part of your revision, add necessary punctuation wherever it is needed. Label the paragraph *Coordinate Elements,* and hand it in to your instructor.

Lesson 17

Apposition and Illustration

When you write about people, objects, or ideas, you usually name them in the first sentence, and then you may use equivalent nouns in other sentences to identify them further as you did in Lesson 2 in this text:

> Jeremy Wills takes full responsibility for the sinking of the cruise ship.
> He is captain of the cruise ship.
> The cruise ship is the *Island Dream.*

In the preceding example *Jeremy Wills* and *captain* represent the same person, and *cruise ship* and *Island Dream* represent the same ship. Using these equivalent nouns ties the sentences together, but the repetition of *cruise ship* three times makes the sentences boring because the repetition is unnecessary. To streamline the sentences, delete the unnecessary words:

> X   Jeremy Wills **/** takes full responsibility for the sinking of the cruise ship **/** .
> **/,/**   ~~He is~~ the captain ~~of the cruise ship.~~   **/,/**
> ~~The cruise ship is the~~ *Island Dream.*

The words remaining are *captain* and *Island Dream,* two nouns. You can combine the remaining words by placing *captain* after *Jeremy Wills* to identify him further and *Island Dream* after *cruise ship* to identify it more specifically:

> Jeremy Wills, the **captain,** takes full responsibility for the sinking of the cruise ship *Island Dream.*

When you place a noun such as *captain* immediately after *Jeremy Wills,* you place *captain* in apposition (placed side by side) with *Jeremy Wills. Captain* may then be identified as an appositive.

Placing a word or a word group in apposition with another word or word group is a way to clarify a term or an idea by adding explanatory information immediately after it. In addition, you make your writing cohesive by eliminating unnecessary words and focusing on the idea to be emphasized.

NOUNS IN APPOSITION

When you place one noun in apposition with another noun, each pair will be in one of three relationships.

1. In the first relationship you use two definite nouns or phrases. For example, you can write *my father,* indicating a particular person, and then place his name, Keith Kellogg, immediately afterwards. Each noun names the same specific person:

> X   The President appointed **my father** / to a diplomatic post in Washington. ~~My father is~~ **Keith Kellogg.**
>
> The President appointed **my father, Keith Kellogg,** to a diplomatic post in Washington.

In the preceding example the writer emphasizes his relationship to Keith Kellogg by identifying him first as *my father.* By reversing the order of the two nouns in the next example, the emphasis is, first, on the man *Keith Kellogg* and, second, on his relationship to the writer:

> X   **Keith Kellogg** / will leave for Washington next week. ~~Keith Kellogg is~~ **my father.**
>
> **Keith Kellogg, my father,** will leave for Washington next week.

You can also expand this sentence by placing *my father* in an adjective clause, but *who is* does not usually improve the sentence because it adds unnecessary words. The adjective clause is not an appositive; it is a modifier:

> *Noun - - - - - - Adjective - - - - - -*
> **Keith Kellogg, who is my father,** will leave for Washington next week.

The next example shows two specific phrases naming the same person:

> X   **The Man of the Year** / will receive his award at a banquet. ~~The Man of the Year is~~ the **Mayor of Toledo.**
>
> **The Man of the Year, the Mayor of Toledo,** will receive his award at a banquet.

2. In the second relationship you write, first, an indefinite noun or phrase that is identified by the noun or phrase following it. In the next sentence *one of his friends* limits the number of people to those who are Jules' friends, but the phrase is less specific than *Carlotta Williams,* a particular person. The name is necessary to tell readers which friend Jules expects to visit:

> Jules expects to visit **one of his friends, Carlotta Williams.**

Sometimes two or more nouns in apposition explain a noun. In the following example *a fractured right arm and a ruptured spleen* explain the kinds of injuries Muriel suffered:

In last week's auto accident, Muriel suffered serious injuries, **a fractured right arm and a ruptured spleen.**

A word that defines another word can be placed in apposition. *Cut* defines *lacerations* in the following example, and *bruises* defines *contusions:*

She also suffered lacerations and contusions, **cuts and bruises,** about her face and neck.

Commas enclose the appositives in the preceding examples because they give additional information about the specific nouns or phrases they rename.

If the appositive consists of three or more words separated by commas, you probably should use dashes before and after the appositives to help readers see where the series begins and ends:

People injured in accidents want first aid from trained personnel—**doctors, nurses,** and **paramedics**—to avoid further injury or complications.

3. In the third relationship a general term or phrase is followed by a more specific noun or phrase that restricts or limits the general term to one particular person, object, or idea. The general terms may be *actor, number, speaker, year, friend,* and others. They may be limited by specific nouns following them: *the actor Dale Robbins, the number ten, the speaker Shelly Carlson, the year 1930, her friend Bonnie.* In the following sentence *the financial adviser* could be any of a number of people. It is only after the specific name appears that readers know which financial adviser the writer means:

   X   The **financial adviser /** listed current stocks to buy.
   ~~The financial adviser is~~ **Charles Hyatt.**

   The financial adviser Charles Hyatt listed current stocks to buy.

Other examples:

   X   Lori likes the **number /** .
   ~~The number is~~ **five.**

   Lori likes **the number five.**

   X   The **speaker /** amused the audience with his stories.
   ~~The speaker is~~ **Charles Kelly.**

   The speaker Charles Kelly amused the audience with his stories.

No commas enclose the appositives in the preceding sentences because the appositives are specific terms that limit or restrict the general term or phrase to one person, object, or idea.

An appositive can be a noun clause that explains a general term such as *suggestion, mystery, reason,* and others:

X   The reason **/** is a mystery.
Belle moved away.

The reason **(that) Belle moved away** is a mystery.

X   Tom made the suggestion **/** .
Members get a discount on admission to the fair.

Tom made the suggestion **that members get a discount on admission to the fair.**

EXERCISE 17A

Combine the following sets of sentences. First, cross out the unnecessary words. Then place the remaining noun after the noun it renames in the base sentence. In some cases the sentences may be combined in more than one way, as the example below indicates. Add punctuation only if the appositive does not restrict or limit the noun it renames as in the example on the right.

EXAMPLE: X   The rock singer **/** wore gaudy costumes.
~~The rock singer was~~ Hare Brain.

The rock singer **Hare Brain** wore gaudy costumes.

X   Hare Brain **/** wore gaudy costumes.
~~Hare Brain was~~ the rock singer.

Hare Brain, **the rock singer,** wore gaudy costumes.

EXAMPLE: Hare Brain, ~~who was~~ a rock singer, wore gaudy costumes.

Hare Brain, **a rock singer,** wore gaudy costumes.

1.   Women admired the Chamber of Commerce president, who was the handsomest man in town.

2.   The bread contains six ingredients.
One ingredient is freshly ground whole wheat flour.
The second and third ingredients are honey and oil.
The last three ingredients are salt, water, and yeast.

3.   The widow proudly showed visitors an old china bowl.
The old china bowl was a replica of one in the British Museum.

4. Jan worked hard for the third prize, which was an old map of China.

5. The apartment owner insisted that the old couple move out.
   The apartment owner was an old man.
   The old man was suspicious.
   The old man was stingy.

6. Police found evidence in a shallow grave.
   The evidence was a skeleton.
   The evidence was a gold ring.

7. The lawyer prepared the wills for his clients.
   The lawyer was Walt Bricker.
   One client was Jessie Young.
   The other client was Brad Franklin.

USING CONNECTORS TO INDICATE APPOSITION

Connectors such as in other words, namely, and that is can link a word or word group with an appositive. Though these connectors can link equivalents effectively, you will learn later in this lesson that today's writers prefer to use punctuation instead.

In the first sentence in other words introduces an explanation that restates the first idea in different words:

> Celia refused to associate with Roger; **in other words,** she would not work in the same office with him.

Namely (or that is) usually follows a general term or idea. It may introduce a synonym that renames a term. It is enclosed in commas:

> The fashion models wanted fewer working hours, **namely (that is),** a five-hour day.

Or it may introduce an independent clause that explains the general term or idea. A semicolon then follows the first independent clause, and a comma follows namely:

> The fashion models wanted fewer working hours; **namely (that is),** they wanted a five-hour day.

Colon and Dash

Today's writers prefer to use the colon (:) or dash (—) instead of <u>namely</u> or <u>that is</u> to introduce a list or an explanation; they believe the words are unnecessary. The colon is a more formal mark of punctuation than the dash:

> The principal listed ten books children should not read: five novels, three short stories, and two science books.

> The woman felt unwanted—she felt everyone ignored her.

Sometimes a list following a colon consists of nouns, each of which is followed by another noun or word group in apposition. Commas appear between each pair, and semicolons separate the pairs. All the nouns in apposition in the following sentence appear in bold type:

> Natalie purchased new clothes for her vacation: two **swimsuits, one** blue and **one** light green; three inexpensive **dresses, all** cotton; one dinner **dress,** a pink **crepe;** and a dozen **shorts** and **tops** to mix and match.

When you use a colon to introduce a list or an explanation, the colon should appear at the end of an independent clause, just as a period does. The colon, however, does not end a sentence but introduces a list or an explanation after the independent clause. In some cases the independent clause might end with <u>the following</u> or <u>as follows.</u> If you place the colon between the verb and its object or complement, you create two fragments, parts of sentences:

Fragment - - - - - - - - *Fragment* - - - - - - - - - - - - -
Not: The teacher ordered: pencils, crayons, and chalk.

Independent clause - - - - - - - - - - - *Appositive* - - - - - - - - - - -
But: The teacher ordered the following: pencils, crayons, and chalk.

Sentence -
Or: The teacher ordered pencils, crayons, and chalk.

Fragment - - - - - - - - - - - *Fragment* - - - - - - - - -
Not: The supplies needed are: paper, ink, and paste.

Sentence -
But: The supplies needed are paper, ink, and paste.

For Example, For Instance

<u>For example</u> sometimes introduces a term or an explanation that restates the first idea in different words. In the following sentence *oranges and grapefruit* rename *citrus fruit salad:*

> The twins prefer a citrus fruit salad, **for example,** oranges and grapefruit.

For example or for instance can also introduce an illustration or an example in a paragraph. In the following sentence the terms *ambassador, Undersecretary of State,* and *governor* illustrate the general term **positions** by giving specific details in the following sentence:

> *Illustration:* Oleg Swenson has held high government positions in the last ten years; **for example,** he served as ambassador to India for a year; he was Undersecretary of State for four years; **AND** he spent the past three years as governor of his state.

EXERCISE 17B

Combine the following sets of sentences, using connectors such as in other words, namely, that is, and for example and appropriate punctuation. Or use colons or dashes to introduce a list or an explanation.

EXAMPLE: X   Roger ordered parts for his car.   */,/*
     /namely,/   ~~Roger ordered~~ a carburetor.   */,/*
               ~~Roger ordered~~ a water pump.   */,/*
    /AND/   ~~Roger ordered~~ a set of spark plugs.

Roger ordered parts for his car, **namely, a carburetor, a water pump, AND a set of spark plugs.**

Or: Roger ordered parts for his car: **a carburetor, a water pump, AND a set of spark plugs.**

Or: Roger ordered parts for his car—**a carburetor, a water pump, AND a set of spark plugs.**

1.   X   Candy wanted detailed reference material in her library.   */,/*
   /in other words,/   She wanted an encyclopedia.

2.   Gardeners can plant two kinds of beans.
         The two kinds of beans are bush beans and pole beans.

3.   The new luggage belonged to the college graduate.
         One piece of luggage was a garment bag.
         A second piece of luggage was a cosmetic case.
         A third piece of luggage was a Pullman case on wheels.

4.   Clarissa likes to visit museums to look at women's costumes from certain periods in history.
She likes dresses with huge skirts from the 1860s.
She likes Victorian dresses of the 1880s.
She likes dresses the flappers wore in the 1920s.

5.   Paolo has a dream.
He wants to return to Venice.
Venice is his home.

6.   The director has chosen the cast for the melodrama.
Donna Taylor will be the heroine.
Ward Cummings will be the hero.
Dell King will be the villain.

7.   Some children face living with permanent handicaps.
Some children have serious mental and physical disabilities.

8.   The farmer raised four grains on his ranch.
One grain was wheat.
A second grain was rice.
A third grain was barley.
A fourth grain was rye.

KEEPING SENTENCE ELEMENTS
PARALLEL OR EQUAL

When you combine several sentences into one, you must be sure that you are joining words or word groups that are the same grammatically. In other words, you can join three or four nouns with the conjunction AND, but you cannot join an adjective and a noun or a verb and a noun with AND. The words or word groups joined by AND must be *equal* or *parallel* to one another; they must be all nouns or all verbs or all adjectives. Given below are three sentences that can be combined. Notice, however, that the first combined sentence is unacceptable because you cannot place the adjectives *enthusiastic* and *energetic* in a series with the noun *quarterback* because adjectives are not parallel with nouns:

SINGLE SENTENCES	COMBINED SENTENCES
The football player is **enthusiastic**. ~~The football player is~~ **energetic**. ~~The football player is~~ a **quarterback**.	*Not:* The football player is **enthusiastic, energetic,** and a **quarterback**. *But:* The football player is an **enthusiastic, energetic quarterback**. *Or:* The football player, a **quarterback**, is **enthusiastic** and **energetic**.

If you try to make a series of two adjectives and the predicate of a sentence, the parts of the series are not equal or parallel because you cannot mix grammatical constructions, as in the following example:

Hector is **reliable**. ~~Hector is~~ **thorough**. ~~Hector~~ / He / **does his job well**.	*Not:* Hector is **reliable, thorough,** and **does his job well**. *But:* Hector is **reliable** and **thorough** **AND he does his job well**.

In the preceding example the first two sentences can be combined, making the two adjectives *reliable* and *thorough* parallel in one independent clause. Then the second sentence is connected to the first with a comma and AND.

EXERCISE 17C

Combine the following sets of sentences. First, read all of the sentences in a set. Second, place X before the base sentence. Third, decide which word groups are the same grammatically—nouns, verbs, phrases, or clauses. Fourth, draw a line through unnecessary words to be deleted. Fifth, combine the sentences, using connectors and changing words or word groups to make them parallel. If you prefer to change some of the sentences to dependent clauses, you may do so.

EXAMPLE: */,/*   ~~Sylvia is~~ an art teacher.   */,/*
         X   Sylvia / spends several hours a week painting landscapes / .
   /AND/   ~~Sylvia spends several hours a week~~ teaching art classes.

       Sylvia, **an art teacher,** spends several hours a week painting landscapes **AND** teaching art classes.

1.   */,/*   Stan is Debbie's brother-in-law.   */,/*
     X   Stan / smokes two packs of cigarettes a day / .   */,/*
       Stan drinks a six-pack of beer / .   */,/*
   /AND/   Stan gambles every chance he gets.

2.   Gordon plans to paint the house.
            Gordon plans to prune the trees.
            Gordon is a dentist.
            He will have a vacation soon.

3.   Celia met her friends at the airport.
            Her friends were former neighbors.
            She drove the friends to her home.

4.   Tomatoes grew tall in the greenhouse.
            The tomatoes were the San Marzano variety.
            They produced an oval-shaped fruit.

EXERCISE 17D

The following sentences are poorly written because they contain words or word groups that are not parallel with other words in the sentence. Complete the revision in the following steps: 1. Read the sentence. 2. Break the sentence apart by writing each idea in it in a separate sentence. 3. Place X before the base sentence. 4. Cross out repeated words in the set of sentences. Then combine the sentences and make elements parallel.

EXAMPLE: Sid listens carefully to the presentation of the plan, thinks about the plan and he offers his suggestions. He is a consulting engineer.

        X Sid **/** listens carefully to the presentation of the plan **/** .   **/,/**
           ~~Sid~~ thinks about the plan **/** .   **/,/**
/AND/ ~~He~~ offers his suggestions.
   /,/ ~~Sid is~~ a consulting engineer.   **/,/**

Sid, **a consulting engineer,** listens carefully to the presentation of the plan, thinks about the plan, **AND** offers his suggestions.

Or: Sid, **a consulting engineer,** listens carefully to the presentation of the plan, he thinks about the plan, **AND** he offers his suggestions.

1. The buyer is experienced, knowledgeable, and has the respect of the employees. He is a man of about forty-five.

2. Sandra is witty, intelligent, and an entertaining actor and folk singer.

3. The people at the town meeting supported the mayor's proposal for increased police protection immediately, enthusiastically, and placed the measure on the ballot.

4. Dave Asher acted responsibly, sympathetically, and settled the claim quickly. He is
   manager of the downtown car wash.

ASSIGNMENT: Apposition

Write a paragraph in which you have eight to ten sentences in the completed version.
Choose a subject that will allow you to place nouns in apposition to one another. For
example, you might write about a person and use his or her titles or roles as appositives. Also include details about the kinds of jobs the person does or the activities he
or she participates in. Begin by writing down your ideas. Then examine your sentences,
and combine those in which you have nouns representing the same person, object, or
idea. Combine any other sentences that can be joined logically. Finally, add necessary
punctuation. Label the paragraph *Apposition,* and hand it in to your instructor.

Review

I. Combining Sentences

   (49 points—7 points each)   SCORE _____

Combine the following sentences by using the techniques you have studied up to this point in this text. Pay special attention to changing some sentences to appositives and making subjects and verbs agree.

1. Don Quixote was Cervantes' hero.
     Don Quixote believed something.
     The windmills were giants.
     He had to destroy the giants.
     Many people today are looking closely at windmills.
     Windmills may be a possible way to generate inexpensive electricity.

2. Nell Warren has been thinking seriously about building a windmill to generate electricity.
     Nell Warren is an accountant.
     Bob Starkey has been thinking seriously about building a windmill to generate electricity.
     Bob Starkey is an auto mechanic.
     Wind seems to blow constantly through their small community of about 2,000 people.

3. A friend of theirs has also expressed interest.
    A friend of theirs is Ted Johnson.

4. Nell remembers something well.
    Bob remembers something well.
    Ted remembers something well.
    Farms in the area had windmills for pumping water.

5. Nell is discovering something.
    Bob is discovering something.
    Ted is discovering something.
    Building a windmill today is extremely expensive.

6. They are learning something.
    Windmill-pumped water can be stored.
    Windmill-generated electricity is available only when the wind is blowing.

7. Nell has decided to reduce her electric bill by using less electricity.
    Bob has decided to reduce his electric bill by using less electricity.
    Ted has decided to reduce his electric bill by using less electricity.

II. Parallelism
   (16 points—4 points each)   SCORE _____

Combine the following sets of sentences. First, read all of the sentences in a set. Second, place X before the base sentence. Third, decide which word groups are the same grammatically—nouns, verbs, phrases, or clauses. Fourth, draw a line through words to be deleted. Fifth, combine the sentences, using connectors and changing words or word groups to make them parallel. If you prefer to change some of the sentences to dependent clauses, you may do so.

1. Tania was in college.
   Each year she sent her grandmother a birthday card.
   Each year she sent her grandmother a Christmas gift.
   She called her grandmother once a month.

2. Maryellen recently met Brad Bellamy.
   Brad is a well-known athlete.
   He has won several golf trophies.
   He has earned about $50,000 this year.

3. Fred specializes in making beef stew.
   Fred is an amateur chef.
   He carefully selects all the ingredients.
   Fred selects five fresh vegetables.
   He selects lean beef.
   He selects several herbs and spices.

4. The mayor met John Weeks.
   The members of the council met John Weeks.
   Three judges met John Weeks.
   John Weeks is a United Nations delegate.
   He is from England.
   They had invited him to visit their city.

III. Writing Sentences
   (35 points—7 points each)   SCORE _____

Use the words or punctuation given in parentheses in sentences.

1. (namely)

2. (<u>that is</u>)

3. (colon :)

4. (dash or dashes —)

5. (<u>for example</u>)

Show these sentences to your instructor or tutor.

Unit 5

Combining Sentences by Transforming Elements

Three techniques you have used in exercises in this text for relating ideas closely and tying sentences together are using connectors between and among sentences, deleting unnecessary words, and embedding word groups. All of these techniques are demonstrated in the following examples:

> Lela was sleeping soundly.
> She did not hear Nelson leave about three in the morning.

> Lela was sleeping soundly; **as a result,** she did not hear Nelson leave about three in the morning.

> Lela did not hear Nelson leave about three in the morning **BECAUSE** she was sleeping soundly.

> Lela, **who was sleeping soundly,** did not hear Nelson leave about three in the morning.

Changing the dependent clause to *sound sleeper* and placing it in apposition with Lela reduces the number of words and makes the sentence compact without changing the meaning noticeably:

> Lela, **a sound sleeper,** did not hear Nelson leave about three in the morning.

In this unit you will continue to make your writing cohesive, but you will use another technique that requires additional steps. You will continue to delete unnecessary words from sentences, but you will also transform (change) some words from one form and function to another to combine the sentences. Using the sentences above, for example, you can make the following transformations to combine them. First, delete *Lela was.* Then place *sleeping soundly* before or after *Lela:*

> ~~Lela was~~ sleeping soundly.
> Lela did not hear Nelson leave about three in the morning.
>
> **Sleeping soundly,** Lela did not hear Nelson leave about three in the morning.
> *Or:* Lela, **sleeping soundly,** did not hear Nelson leave about three in the morning.

The word *sleeping* in the sentence appears without the auxiliary verb *was.* A verb form used in this way is called a **verbal.** It may be used by itself or in a phrase, a word group without a subject or verb, and it functions as a noun or a modifier. Transforming verbs to verbals allows you to write compact and meaningful sentences that make their points effectively and economically. In the lessons that follow you will learn about the characteristics and function of verbals and verbal phrases and how to use them in combining sentences.

To prepare yourself for these lessons on verbal phrases, you should first review Lesson 5 on verb tenses to help you remember the parts of the verbs that are used alone or with auxiliary verbs to form the verb tenses. The parts that you will be working with in these lessons are Part 5 (V-ing), also called a present participle or gerund; Part 4 (V-ed), also called a past participle; and Part 1 (Base) to form the infinitive.

The V-ing Verbal Phrase

When you want to show that an event or an action continues over a period of time, you use a form of the verb *be (am, is, are, was, were, been)* together with a main verb ending in *-ing* to form a **verb** phrase that functions as the verb in the sentence:

> The writer **is publishing** his stories himself.
> He **has been writing** stories about his personal experiences for at least twenty years.
> Friends who wanted to read the stories **had been asking** him to put them in print.

In addition, most V-ing forms can be used without the auxiliary verb as nouns, adjectives, or adverbs. Compare the following sentences. The verb in each sentence on the left below consists of an auxiliary verb and the V-ing form, for example, *is howling.* The verb becomes a verbal by dropping the auxiliary verb—*is* or *was*—and using the verbal in another sentence as an adjective, adverb, or noun in the sentences on the right:

VERBS	VERBALS	
The wind **is howling.**	*Adj:*	The **howling** wind sounds mournful.
Sylvia **was packing** her suitcase.	*Adv:*	Sylvia spent an hour **packing.**
Pete **was running** today.	*Noun:*	Pete enjoys **running** every day.
The child **was crying.**	*Noun:*	The child's **crying** irritated his father.

EXERCISE 18A

All of the following sentences contain verbs, and some of them also contain V-ing verbals. Underline the verb or verb phrase in each sentence. Then write the verb in the first blank. If you also find verbals in the sentences, underline the verbals, and write them in the second blank.

	VERB	V-ING VERBAL
EXAMPLE: Sam <u>was cleaning</u> the apartment for an hour.	was cleaning	
San <u>spent</u> an hour <u>cleaning</u> the apartment.	spent	cleaning
The <u>crackling</u> fire <u>is burning</u> brightly.	is burning	crackling
The <u>burning</u> logs <u>crackle</u> constantly.	crackle	burning

1. The turkey has been smoking in the cooker for an hour. _____ _____

2. The smoking chimney adds irritating pollutants to the air. _____ _____

3. Shizuko is saving money for the camping trip. _____ _____

4. Jeffrey likes saving pieces of string. _____ _____

5. Fishing is a peaceful pastime for many people. _____ _____

6. Jan was working ten hours a day as a purchasing agent. _____ _____

7. Tom spends his days working in the nursery. _____ _____

8. The complaining man is disturbing everyone. _____ _____

V-ING VERBAL PHRASES

A verbal phrase is the verbal and the words that complete and modify it. Like verbals, verbal phrases may function as adjectives, adverbs, and nouns. The following examples show sentences with verbal phrases, and the labels before the sentences identify how each phrase functions:

Adj: The old couple, **walking slowly along the sandy beach,** enjoyed the sunny day.

Adj: They stopped occasionally, **giving bread to the hungry sea gulls.**

Adv: They spent the day **listening to the waves break on the shore.**

Noun

Subject:	**Walking slowly along the sandy beach** pleased the old couple.
Direct object:	The old couple enjoyed **giving bread to the hungry sea gulls.**
Object of prep:	They relaxed by **listening to the waves break on the shore.**

The following sections explain how you can combine sentences by changing one sentence to a verbal phrase and embedding (inserting) it in the base sentence.

V-ING AS ADJECTIVES

You may combine sentences by changing one to a verbal phrase in the following steps:

1. Read the sentences. Place X before the base sentence.

> X   The small boy struggled up the stairway.
> He **was carrying** a large bundle of clothing.

2. Delete unnecessary words, and change the verb to a verbal.

> The small boy struggled up the stairway.
> ~~He was~~ **carrying** a large bundle of clothing.

Carrying a large bundle of clothing is a verbal phrase. Because *he was* has been deleted, the word group is no longer a sentence; it is a fragment, only a part of a sentence. It has been transformed into a phrase that must be embedded in a sentence.

3. Embed the verbal phrase in the base sentence.

> **Carrying a large bundle of clothing,** the small boy struggled up the stairway.
> *Or:* The small boy, **carrying a large bundle of clothing,** struggled up the stairway.

The verbal phrase in the sentence above functions as an adjective, telling more about the small boy. An adjective verbal phrase, like any other adjective modifier, should be placed immediately before or after the noun it modifies. However, an adjective verbal phrase that modifies the subject can appear at the end of the sentence if there is no other noun in the sentence:

> The small boy slipped, **momentarily losing his balance.**

In the following example, you can change the verb *rang* in the first sentence to the verbal *ringing* in order to combine the sentences:

> ringing
> ~~The small boy **rang**~~ the doorbell.

> X   The small boy waited for his uncle.

The verbal phrase *ringing the doorbell* can be placed before or after *boy,* but probably not at the end of the sentence because it seems to modify *uncle* and indicate that the uncle was ringing the doorbell:

> **Ringing the doorbell,** the small boy waited for his uncle.
> The small boy, **ringing the doorbell,** waited for his uncle.
> *Not:* The small boy waited for his uncle, **ringing the doorbell.**

You could also combine the preceding pair of sentences in the following way:

> The small boy, **who was ringing the doorbell,** waited for his uncle.

However, there is no advantage in using *who was;* the meaning is clear without the extra words and the sentence more easily readable with the verbal phrase.

When you read the following set of sentences, you can note that they are short and choppy. However, if you change three of them to verbal phrases and embed them in the base sentence, you have improved the presentation of the information greatly. Before you change verbs to verbals and combine the sentences, you have to consider carefully what the set of sentences is saying. In reading the sentences that follow, you should determine that the second sentence about finding the calf is the main idea in relation to the other sentences. The second sentence, therefore, becomes the base sentence, and the other sentences are embedded in it:

> Three ranchers ~~were~~ **riding** in a jeep.
> X ~~They~~ found a sick calf.
> ~~It~~ **was lying** behind a large bush.
> ~~It~~ **was gasping** for breath.
>
> Three ranchers, **riding in a jeep,** found a sick calf, **lying behind a large bush and gasping for breath.**

Commas enclose verbal phrases that modify specific terms:

> Tim Hewitt, **standing over there talking to his brother,** plans to run for mayor.

No commas enclose verbal phrases needed to identify a general term:

> The man **wearing the brown shirt** plans to run for mayor.   (Which man? The man wearing the brown shirt . . .)

V-ING AS NOUNS

The adjective verbal phrases in the preceding examples modify nouns and tell which one. Verbal phrases can also function as nouns in sentences. In the following examples the V-ing verbals function as subject, object, object of the preposition, and appositive. If you read two or three sentences you have written and believe that the relationship of ideas is closer than the sentences would indicate, think about combining the sentences. In the first example, the two sentences on the left are satisfactory, but the combined sentence helps the readers see more quickly and directly that the ticking of the clock caused Maurice's nervousness. You will note a similar result in the other sentences that follow:

SINGLE SENTENCES	COMBINED SENTENCES	
The clock was ticking. This made Maurice nervous.	*Subject:*	**The ticking of the clock** made Maurice nervous.
The owner enjoyed something. He operated his scale-model steam engine for children on weekends.	*Object:*	The owner enjoyed **operating his scale-model steam engine for children on weekends.**
The men and women entertained themselves. They floated down the river in a raft.	*Object of prep:*	The men and women entertained themselves by **floating down the river in a raft.**
Ms. Peterson enjoyed her work. Her work was preparing manuscripts for publication.	*Appositive:*	Ms. Peterson enjoyed her work, **preparing manuscripts for publication.**

Notice that when the verbal phrase functions as a subject, object, or object of the preposition, you do not need a comma because the phrase functions as a noun in the sentence.

EXERCISE 18B

Combine the following sets of sentences by changing one or more sentences to verbal phrases and embedding them in the base sentence.

separating

EXAMPLE: X   Max stopped the fight.   ~~He separated~~ the two boys.

Max stopped the fight by **separating the two boys.**

trying

X   The teenager fell off the roof of the barn.   ~~He tried~~ to rescue the frightened kitten.

The teenager, **trying to rescue the frightened kitten,** fell off the roof of the barn.

1. The traveler found no food in the cupboard.   The traveler went to a restaurant for lunch.

2. Carla dislikes something.   She sets her hair every night.

3. The children were trying to confuse the new teacher.   They changed seats in the classroom.

4. Gene held his throbbing head.   He was moaning softly.   He searched unsuccessfully for aspirins.

5. Mary prefers something.   She cooks meat in a pressure cooker.

6. Boris moved to Texas.   This was a new adventure for Boris.

7. The door leads to a small room.   The door has been locked for many years.

8. The chairman of the committee spoke loudly.   He banged the table.   He told everyone to listen to him.

V-ING AS ADVERBS

The V-ing verbal can be used as an adverb that tells *where* or *how* following the verbs *go* and *spend:*

> Five people went **hunting for a lion.**   (Went where? *hunting...*)
> They spent hours **looking for the lion.**   (Spent hours how? *looking...*)

V-ing can also be a part of an adverbial modifier that begins with the connectors WHILE, BEFORE, AFTER, SINCE, and WHEN. This modifier can develop by combining sentences if the subject of two sentences is the same:

> X   The hunters walked through the woods for hours.
> The hunters were looking for a mountain lion.

First, change the second sentence to an adverbial clause by using the connector WHILE before it:

> The hunters walked through the woods for hours **WHILE they were looking for a mountain lion.**

Then change the adverbial clause to an adverbial phrase by deleting *they were.* The modifier can appear before or after the base sentence:

> The hunters walked through the woods for hours **WHILE looking for a mountain lion.**
> **WHILE looking for a mountain lion,** the hunters walked through the woods for hours.

EXERCISE 18C

Combine the following sentences if the subjects in both sentences are the same by changing one of the sentences to a V-ing adverbial modifier. First, place X before the base sentence. Next, change the other sentence to a dependent clause by using connectors such as WHILE, SINCE, WHEN, BEFORE, and AFTER. Then delete the subject of the dependent clause, and change the verb to a V-ing verbal. Finally, combine the sentences. If the subjects are not the same, use an appropriate connector, and add punctuation where it is needed.

EXAMPLE: X   Dan finished typing two letters.

       /BEFORE/   ~~Then~~ he opened the day's mail.

      Adv. clause: Dan finished typing two letters **BEFORE he opened the day's mail.**

      Adv. V-ing: Dan finished typing two letters **BEFORE opening the day's mail.**

      Or: **BEFORE opening the day's mail,** Dan finished typing two letters.

EXAMPLE: X   In the mail Dan found a thousand-dollar check.

       /THAT/   Burt Smith had finally sent ~~the check~~ to repay an old loan.

      Combined: In the mail Dan found a thousand-dollar check **THAT Burt Smith had finally sent to repay an old loan.**

1. /AFTER/   Cary fell from the tree.
         X   Cary slowly struggled to his feet.

2. /BEFORE/   Cary might climb a tree again.
         X Cary would have to check the strength and thickness of the branches.

3.   X Cary had had other accidents.
   /THAT/   The other accidents were the result of his carelessness.

4.   Lydia read a novel.
         She was waiting for her husband to return.

5.   Rosalee left home.
                Her mother immediately rented the bedroom to a college student.

6.   Karen and her friends spent the sunny day in a raft on the river.
                They all had painful sunburns.

7.   Tom was helping a friend move into a new apartment.
                Tom hurt his back badly.

EXERCISE 18D

Connect and combine the following sentences. In some cases you will be able to combine the sentences by changing verbs to verbals that modify nouns. In other cases you will use ways that you have studied in preceding lessons. First, read the sentences in the set. Second, place X before the sentence or sentences that you choose for the base sentence. Third, cross out unnecessary words. Fourth, change the verbs to verbals wherever you can. Fifth, add connectors, or make any other appropriate changes. Finally, combine all the sentences in a set into a single sentence.

EXAMPLE: ~~The pilot was~~ preparing for a flight to Anchorage.   **/, V-ing,/**
              X   The pilot **/** checked weather reports **/** .
      /AND/ ~~He~~ filed a flight plan.

The pilot, **preparing for a flight to Anchorage,** checked weather reports **AND** filed a flight plan.

                     making
EXAMPLE: ~~He made~~ the pre-flight check.   **/V-ing/**
            X ~~It~~ was a routine **/** .
   /(THAT)/ He always followed ~~the routine~~.

Making the pre-flight check was a routine **(THAT)** he always followed.

1.   The pilot was flying in a single-engine plane.   **/, V-ing,/**
     X   He **/** enjoyed the peaceful Alaskan wilderness below him.

2.   The pilot looked out the window.
           He saw snow-covered meadows and hills.
           He saw no people, animals, roads, or buildings.

3.   He began something.
           He worried.
           He wondered where he was.

4.   He heard the plane engine sputter slightly.
           He quickly looked at the gasoline gauge.
           He saw the red indicator on the empty mark.

5.   The pilot felt his heartbeat quicken.
           He told himself not to panic.
           He knew he had to act quickly.

6.   In the distance slightly to the right he saw a thin column of smoke.
           It was rising from the chimney of a large wooden building.

7.   He saw a long path in the snow directly ahead.
           It looked like an airstrip.
           He headed for it.
           He hoped he had enough fuel to carry him there.

8.   The plane engine stopped.
           The plane glided toward the path in the snow.

9.   He came closer.
                He realized the path was not an airstrip.
                People had made the path.
                The people were wearing snowshoes.

10.   The landing gear of the plane sank into the snow.
                The nose of the plane hit the snow embankment.
                The tail of the plane rose straight up and fell forward slowly.

11.   The pilot was hanging upside down in the cockpit.
                He slowly loosened his seat belt.
                He finally managed to get his feet below him.

12.   Hunters ran from the building.
                They pulled open the door of the plane.
                They helped the pilot out.
                They took him to the building.

13.   The next day they took him by dog sled to a train station.
                Soon the pilot was on his way home.
                He was wondering how he could get his plane back.

ASSIGNMENT: V-ing Verbals

Write a paragraph that consists of eight to ten sentences when it is completed. Choose a topic about travel in modern times or in the past. You might discuss modes of transportation, reasons for travel, advantages of travel, or any other aspect of travel that appeals to you. First, write your ideas down in a series of sentences. Then revise what you have written by connecting and combining sentences to show the relationship of ideas clearly. Use V-ing verbals and verbal phrases wherever they are appropriate. Underline the verbals and verbal phrases in your paragraph. Label the paragraph *V-ing Verbals,* and hand it in to your instructor.

The V-ed Verbal Phrase

The second kind of verbal you will learn to use in combining sentences is the V-ed (past participle) form. In Lesson 5 you learned that you use the auxiliary verbs *have* or *has* with V-ed to form the present perfect tense and *had* with V-ed to form the past perfect tense. The following sentences give examples of each one:

> The Robinsons **have bought** the Victorian house on First Street
> The house **has stood** there for ninety-five years.
> The Robinsons **had looked** for a house to restore for at least three years.

In this lesson you will learn to use V-ed as a verbal, but first you will study active and passive verbs because the V-ed verbal is derived from passive verbs.

ACTIVE AND PASSIVE VERBS

You may have observed that sentences consisting of the subject, verb, and direct object represent a common—probably the most common—sentence pattern in English. Such sentences show that the subject affects or does something to the object. The verb is **active.** In the sentence taken from the example above, the Robinsons, the doers, do something to the Victorian house, the receiver of the action. *House* is the direct object (DO):

>   *S*   *V- - - - - - - -*   *DO*
> The Robinsons **have bought** the Victorian house on First Street.

The same idea can be expressed in a different way by making the receiver of the action—the Victorian house—the subject and using a **passive** verb instead of the active verb. To make the change, follow these steps, using the sentence above:

1. Place *Victorian house,* which is the receiver of the action, in the subject position in the sentence.

2. Change the active verb *have bought* to the passive form (PV) by using a form of the verb *be (am, is, are, was, were, been, being)* with V-ed: *has been bought.*
3. Make the subject *the Robinsons* the object of the preposition *by: by the Robinsons.*

```
    S         V--------              DO
The Robinsons have bought the Victorian house on First Street.

         S            PV---------- Pr    OP
The Victorian house on First Street has been bought by the Robinsons.
```

Notice that the verb form changes from *have bought,* used with the plural subject *the Robinsons* in the first sentence above to *has been bought,* used with the singular subject *the Victorian house.*

If the readers do not have to know who bought the house, you can omit *by the Robinsons.* The sentence then reads:

The Victorian house has been bought.

One point to remember is that *passive* does **not** mean *past tense.* Passive verbs may be written in the present, past, future, perfect, and progressive tenses. The following sentences show both active and passive verbs in several tenses:

ACTIVE VERBS	DOER (Subject)	ACTIVE VERB	RECEIVER (Direct Object)
Present:	The Robinsons	are buying	furniture.
Present perfect:	They	have chosen	several antiques.
Future:	The store owner	will deliver	the pieces.

PASSIVE VERBS	RECEIVER (Subject)	PASSIVE VERB	DOER (by OP)
Present:	Furniture	is being bought	by the Robinsons.
Present perfect:	Several antiques	have been chosen	by them.
Future:	The pieces	will be delivered	by the store owner.

Passive verbs are especially useful when you want to emphasize the receiver of the action. However, too many passive verbs make writing impersonal and static because they hide what the subject is doing. If, however, you write technical or scientific reports, you may want to use passive verbs to keep your writing impersonal.

EXERCISE 19A

Rewrite the following sentences by making the verbs passive. First, place the receiver of the action in the subject position. Then change the active verb to the passive form by using a form of the verb *be (am, is, are, was, were, been, being)* with V-ed. Finally, make the subject of the sentence the object of the preposition *by.*

EXAMPLE: Charles and Melinda Robinson made plans to restore the Victorian mansion.

Plans to restore the Victorian mansion were made by Charles and Melinda Robinson.
Or: Plans to restore the Victorian mansion were made.

1. Charles Robinson painted the outside of the old Victorian mansion.

2. He had discovered the original color by scraping away several layers of paint.

3. He found a light tan color on the siding and a dark brown color on the trim.

4. Mel Stauffer at the paint store mixed matching paints.

5. The contrasting colors emphasized the details of the ornate trim.

EXERCISE 19B

Rewrite the following sentences by making the verbs active.

1. The interior of the Victorian mansion was redecorated by Melinda Robinson.

2. The wallpapers and paints were chosen by Melinda to match the originals as closely as possible.

3. The old wallpaper was removed by Melinda with Charles' help.

4. The draperies were made of velvets and brocades by Melinda's sister.

5. The Victorian furniture had been purchased over a period of years by Charles and Melinda.

V-ED VERBALS

If you have a passive verb in a sentence, you can change it to a V-ed verbal by deleting the auxiliary verb. Then you can use the verbal as an adjective to modify a noun in the base sentence:

> ~~The beans~~ **~~were~~ scorched.** Joe would not eat the beans.

> Joe would not eat the **scorched** beans.

> However, Joe enjoyed the potatoes and beef ribs. ~~The potatoes~~ **~~were~~ baked** and ~~the beef ribs~~ **~~were~~ barbecued.**

> Joe enjoyed the **baked** potatoes and the **barbecued** beef ribs.

A few V-ed verbals such as *injured, wounded,* and *forgotten* can be used as nouns:

> Several drivers **were injured.** The **injured** were taken to the hospital.
> Two people **had been wounded** during the shooting. The **wounded** received first aid.
> Old people **are** sometimes **forgotten** by family and friends. The **forgotten** lead lonely lives.

EXERCISE 19C

All of the following sentences contain verbs, and some of them also contain verbals. Underline the verb or verb phrase in each sentence. Then write the verb in the first blank. If you also find a verbal in the sentence, underline it, and write it in the second blank.

	VERB	V-ED VERBAL
EXAMPLE: The plate-glass window <u>was broken</u> by the baseball.	was broken	
The contractor <u>replaced</u> the <u>broken</u> window.	replaced	broken

1. The hidden lake was frozen by the below-zero temperatures.

2. The cake is frosted with strawberry ice cream.

3. The captured burglar had been beaten by the homeowner.

4. The injured child's knee was bruised badly.

5. The prized horse had been stolen by rustlers.

6. The wedding gown will be borrowed
   from a friend.

7. Three people had taken the forbidden
   drug.

8. The prize was given to the amazed
   contestant.

V-ED VERBAL PHRASES

When you combine sentences by changing the verb to a V-ed verbal, the process is the same as combining sentences with the V-ing verbal. The V-ed verbal, functioning as an adjective, should either come before or follow the noun it modifies to keep the meaning of the sentence clear. Commas enclose the verbal phrase in the first example below because it gives extra information about a specific term. The verbal phrase in the second example is not enclosed in commas because *woman* is a general term and the verbal is needed to identify which woman was hired:

> X   Darren **/** continued to arrive late at work almost every morning
> He had been **warned** about his tardiness.   **/, V-ed,/**
>
> Darren, **warned about his tardiness,** continued to arrive late at work almost every morning.
>
> The woman **was hired** the week before.   **/V-ed/**
> X   She could handle Darren's job easily.
>
> The woman **hired the week before** could handle Darren's job easily.

V-ed verbals following verbs such as *become, remain,* and *feel* can sometimes be taken from one sentence and placed in the base sentence to tie the ideas together more closely:

> His employer **became tired** of Darren's lack of responsibility.   **/, V-ed,/**
> X   He decided to fire Darren the next week.
>
> His employer, **tired of Darren's lack of responsibility,** decided to fire Darren the next week.
>
> Darren **felt concerned** about finding another job.   **/, V-ed,/**
> X   He promised to be on time.
>
> Darren, **concerned about finding another job,** promised to be on time.

Sometimes you can change an adverbial clause beginning with ALTHOUGH, WHEN, ONCE, and UNLESS to an adverbial phrase if the subject of both the independent and adverbial clauses is the same. In the following example, *Melanie was* is deleted from the adverbial clause, and *Melanie* replaces *she* in the independent clause:

ALTHOUGH ~~Melanie was~~ tired and uninterested in the conversation, ~~she~~ ^{Melanie} tried to keep her eyes open.

ALTHOUGH **tired** and **uninterested** in the conversation, Melanie tried to keep her eyes open.

WHEN ~~the robber was~~ arrested, ~~he~~ ^{the robber} insisted he was not guilty.

WHEN **arrested,** the robber insisted he was not guilty.

EXERCISE 19D

Connect and combine the following sentences. In some cases you will be able to combine the sentences by changing verbs to verbals. In other cases you will use ways to connect and combine sentences that you have studied in preceding lessons. First, read the sentences in each set. Second, place X before the sentence you choose for the base sentence. Third, cross out unnecessary words. Fourth, change the verbs to verbals wherever you can. Fifth, add connectors, or make any other appropriate changes. Finally, combine all the sentences in a set into a single sentence.

EXAMPLE: X The frozen North **/** seems peaceful and quiet. **/;/**
~~It is~~ covered most of the year by ice and snow. **/, V-ed,/**
/however,/ The ice is actually a destructive force in the form of glaciers.

The frozen North, **covered most of the year by ice and snow,** seems peaceful and quiet; **however,** the ice is actually a destructive force in the form of glaciers.

1.　　　　Glaciers are seen today in Glacier Bay National Monument, Alaska. **/V-ed/**
　　X　Glaciers began forming about 4,000 years ago.
/BECAUSE/　Snow that fell each year did not melt.

2.　　　X　Instead it changed to grains of ice.
/THAT/　The grains of ice gradually fused into enormous masses of solid ice.

3.　　　　These gigantic ice masses moved down mountains.
　　　　They moved like mammoth bulldozers.
　　　　They moved for about 3,000 years.

4.   Deep gorges formed.
   They were carved out by the moving glaciers.

5.   The glaciers stripped the land.
   They carried plants, soil, and rock with them.

6.   The weight of the ice left ridges.
   The abrasive action left ridges.
   The ridges were carved into the rock beneath.

7.   The glacial ice gradually melted.
   It filled the gorges with water.
   The glaciers had carved the gorges.

8.   Huge pieces of ice broke away from the face of the glaciers.
   The huge pieces crashed into the water.
   They caused huge waves.
   They filled the inlets with massive icebergs.

ASSIGNMENT: V-ed Verbals

Choose a topic about one of the sciences—astronomy, biology, botany, chemistry, geology, and physics. If you choose astronomy, you might write something about space exploration. For botany you might discuss the services provided by government agricultural departments or experiments being conducted to improve the quality of particular foods. Write a paragraph that consists of eight to ten sentences when it is completed. First, write your ideas down in a series of sentences. Then revise what you have written by connecting and combining sentences to show the relationship of ideas clearly. Use V-ed verbals and verbal phrases wherever they are appropriate. Underline the V-ed verbals and verbal phrases in your paragraph. Label the paragraph *V-ed Verbals,* and hand it in to your instructor.

Lesson 20

The Infinitive Verbal Phrase

The infinitive, like V-ing and V-ed, functions as a verbal in sentences. It expresses action or existence, and it shows tense just as the verb does. However, it is different from the verb because it does not function as the predicate in a sentence and it does not indicate person (first, second, third) or number (singular, plural):

Verbs, third person singular:	Lewis **teaches** Megan. She **paints** portraits.
Infinitive:	Lewis teaches Megan **to paint** portraits.

The infinitive consists of a form of the verb preceded by *to,* which serves as a marker of the infinitive. Here are the forms of the infinitive:

ACTIVE	PASSIVE
to speak	to be taken
to be guarding	
to have considered	to have been wanted
to have been thinking	

Every sentence must include at least one verb, but it may or may not include infinitives. Yet infinitives are used extensively. If you examine what you say and write, you will find that many of your sentences contain one infinitive, sometimes more.

Infinitives appear after a large number of verbs. Here is a partial list: *begin, continue, like, shock, need, deserve, want, decide, expect, find, urge, force, be, cause, advise, appoint, allow, ask, choose, claim, teach, permit, order, like, require,* and *tell.* Each of the following sentences has at least one verb, and all but two of the sentences have infinitives:

> The dairy farmer had a problem **to solve.** His cows continued **to become** sick and **die** even though the veterinarian had found the feed and water **to be** satisfactory. The farmer wanted **to be told** what was wrong. With further investigation he learned the answer. A blood specialist was able **to find** a toxic chemical in the cows' blood. Then the farmer was shocked **to learn** that a feed company employee had accidentally mixed the toxic chemical into the feed. The result was the poisoning of cows and of the people in the state who had drunk the milk from the cows.

The infinitive may appear in sentences without *to* if the following words are the verbs: *hear, watch, see, help, let, make:*

> The crowd watched the stuntman **fall** out of the wrecked car.
> They heard him **cry** for help.

Infinitives may function as adjectives, adverbs, and nouns in sentences. Like the other verbals, they may be completed by modifiers, objects, and complements. The following examples show infinitives and infinitive phrases:

Adjective:	The person **to call in an emergency** is her husband.
	The child ignores the question **to be answered.**
Adverb:	The driver was foolish **to take the chance.**
	The crowd has been impatient **to hear the news.**
	The tire is easy **to change.**
	The hikers struggle **to climb the mountain.**
Noun	
Subject:	**To own a house** is the couple's dream.
Object:	The couple hopes **to own a house soon.**
	Cheryl decided **to agree to go with John.**
Complement:	The solution is **to invite everyone to the christening.**

The examples above show infinitives with modifiers, objects, and complements. Infinitives may also have subjects:

> The supervisor caused **Harry to lose his job.**
> Jerry wants **the office to be painted by next week.**
> Clara advised **Mary to see a doctor immediately.**

EXERCISE 20A

All of the following sentences contain verbs, and some of them also contain infinitive verbals. Underline the verb or verb phrase in each sentence. Then write the verb in the first blank. If you also find an infinitive verbal in the sentence, underline it, and write it in the second blank.

	VERB	INFINITIVE VERBAL
EXAMPLE: Andrew <u>advised</u> his mother <u>to sell</u> the car.	advised	to sell
1. Michael asked Maureen to complete his biography.	_____	_____
2. Jose intends to go to the convention in March.	_____	_____

	VERB	INFINITIVE VERBAL
3. The harbor pilot was careful to avoid rocks and tree limbs in the bay.	_____	_____
4. The parents did not allow their children to play baseball.	_____	_____
5. The brick wall was built to hide rubbish cans.	_____	_____
6. Jan saw the small boy cut his finger with a razor.	_____	_____
7. The older boys made Tim cry frequently.	_____	_____
8. Marge held the child to keep her from falling.	_____	_____

CHANGING DEPENDENT CLAUSES TO INFINITIVES

The infinitive, like other verbals, enables you to make sentences more compact. By being aware of infinitives, you can sometimes change dependent clauses to infinitive phrases by deleting unnecessary words:

SENTENCES WITH DEPENDENT CLAUSES

Fred hopes ~~that he can~~ **arrive by nine o'clock.**

He wants a car ~~that he can~~ **drive to the convention center.**

He has several problems ~~that need~~ **to be solved before the meeting.**

SENTENCES WITH INFINITIVE PHRASES

Fred hopes **to arrive by nine o'clock.**

He wants a car **to drive to the convention center.**

He has several problems **to be solved before the meeting.**

EXERCISE 20B

You will find a dependent clause in each of the following sentences. Underline the dependent clause, and then rewrite the sentence by changing the dependent clause to an infinitive phrase.

EXAMPLE: The goal is <u>that they win the election</u>.
The goal is **to win the election.**

1. The family pretended that they accepted the court's decision.

2. The inspector hopes that he can convince the miners that dangers are present.

3. Virginia Carson told her publisher that he should spend more for advertising her book.

4. The company president's wife ordered a very expensive ball gown that she will wear to the company's annual dinner dance.

5. Phyllis Holt must find another speaker who can replace her on the panel.

COMBINING SENTENCES WITH INFINITIVES

You may combine sentences by using infinitives in three ways. One is to use an infinitive to express purpose (or tell *why*):

> Jeff needs money. ~~Jeff wants~~ to purchase a car.
>
> Jeff needs money **to purchase a car.**
>
>   to invest
> Lydia will buy the land next to the department store. ~~Lydia's purpose is investing~~ in real
>
>   to sell
> estate. ~~Lydia's purpose is selling~~ for a profit in a few years.
>
> Lydia will buy the land next to the department store **to invest in real estate and to sell for a profit in a few years.**
> *Or:* **To invest in real estate and sell for a profit in a few years,** Lydia will buy the land next to the department store.

The infinitive phrase may also tell *how:*

>   to become
> Jim helped his sons. ~~They became~~ physically fit with regular exercise.
>
> Jim helped his sons **to become physically fit with regular exercise.**

A third way is to use the infinitive as a noun:

>   to answer
> The questions ~~need answers.~~ ~~This~~ requires at least an hour.
>
> **To answer the questions** requires at least an hour.

to receive   to arrive

The supervisor expects ~~something~~. ~~He will receive~~ a reply this afternoon. ~~He will arrive~~ at a decision.

The supervisor expects **to receive a reply this afternoon and to arrive at a decision.**

When you combine the following sentences, you have to supply a subject for the infinitives by changing *he* to *him:*

him to gain   him to feel

John's constant eating caused ~~this~~. ~~He gained~~ weight. ~~He felt~~ ill most of the time.

John's constant eating caused **him to gain weight and to feel ill most of the time.**

EXERCISE 20C

Combine the following sets of sentences in these steps. Place X before the base sentence. Then change the other sentence(s) to infinitive phrases and attach them to the base sentence.

EXAMPLE: X   The sergeant received orders **/** .
                ~~He was~~ to evacuate the area immediately.   **/Inf/**

             The sergeant received orders **to evacuate the area immediately.**

to settle

EXAMPLE: **/** The children's arguments ~~needed settling~~.   **/Inf/**
          X   ~~This~~ required patience.

          To settle the children's arguments required patience.

1. X   Janice ran through the airline terminal.
        She wanted to catch the plane.   **/Inf/**

2.   Shari helped Richard.
        He made the critical decision that changed his life.

3.   The renter was shocked.
        She had received an eviction notice from the landlord.

4.   Otto expected this.
        He was to travel to Germany immediately.
        He was to open a branch office for his company.

5.   Martin's unwise actions caused this.
        He lost his job.
        He lost his wife.
        He lost his best friend.

6.   The plant manager wanted to explain his company's policy.
        He wanted to get support for bringing workers from out of state.
        The plant manager spoke to local residents at a town meeting.

MISPLACED MODIFIERS

When you studied adjectives (Lesson 3) and adjective clauses (Lesson 14), you
learned that these modifiers must be placed as close to the noun that they modify
as possible because adjectives tend to modify the nearest noun. If the adjective
modifiers are misplaced, the meaning of the sentence may be unclear. The only
way to clarify meaning is to rewrite the sentence, placing the modifier where it
belongs. The correction symbol *MM* is often used to indicate a misplaced modifier.

Misplaced Verbal Phrases

When verbal phrases function as modifiers, you must also take care to place them as
close to the word they modify as possible. If you do not, the sentence may be wrong-
ly interpreted. For example, if you combine the sentences on the left in the usual
way, you then have a combined sentence like the one on the right. The most likely
interpretation is that Judy was driving to work with a new friend when Dan saw her.
The sentence does not indicate clearly whether Judy or the friend was driving:

> Dan saw Judy.   Dan saw Judy with a new friend, driving to work.
> Judy was with a new friend.
> They were driving to work.

By placing *driving* next to *Judy,* you can indicate much more clearly that she was the
driver:

> Dan saw Judy, who was driving to work with a new friend.
> Dan saw Judy, driving to work with a new friend.

However, if you want to say that Dan was the one driving to work, you can rewrite the sentence in these ways:

> While driving to work, Dan saw Judy with a new friend.
> *Or:* Dan, driving to work, saw Judy with a new friend.

If you find a sentence that seems confusing in a paragraph you have written, you can examine it by breaking it into its basic parts. In the first example, the V-ed verbal phrase *seated in the plane* does not seem to belong at the beginning of the sentence:

> **Seated in the plane,** the flight attendants served dinner to the passengers.

To decide where the V-ed verbal phrase belongs, write the verbal phrase down:

> seated in the plane

Then ask who was or were seated in the plane. Write the answer before *seated.* You now have a sentence:

> The passengers were seated in the plane.

Then write the second part of the sentence as a separate sentence:

> The flight attendants served dinner to the passengers.

Finally, combine the two sentences in the usual way, and you will be able to place the verbal phrase after *passengers:*

> ~~The passengers were~~ seated in the plane.   **/, V-ed/**
> X   The flight attendants served dinner to the passengers **/** .

> The flight attendants served dinner to the passengers, **seated in the plane.**

Misplaced Prepositional Phrases

Prepositional phrases are modifiers that must also be placed as close to the word they modify as possible. In the following sentence, for example, the prepositional phrase *in a red bikini* seems to modify *poodle.* You can examine the sentence by breaking it into its basic parts:

> The long-legged model walked her poodle **in a red bikini.**   (Who wore the red bikini? The long-legged model.)

> ~~The long-legged model was~~ in a red bikini.
> X   The long-legged model **/** walked her poodle.

> The long-legged model **in a red bikini** walked her poodle.

In the next example, *As a consultant* seems to modify *the company:*

> **As a consultant,** the company gave Otis Washington the authority to reassign personnel. (Who was the consultant? Otis Washington.)

In the revision, you may find it better to make *consultant* an appositive that renames *Otis Washington:*

<del>Otis Washington acted</del> **as** a consultant.

X   The company gave Otis Washington
/   the authority to reassign personnel.

The company gave Otis Washington, **its consultant,** the authority to reassign personnel.

Two Modifiers

If you write a sentence with two or more word groups that are supposed to modify the same noun, you may find that the second modifier appears to modify the noun closest to it. In the following example, *with the bad sunburn* seems to modify *pool:*

> The teenager in the pool with the bad sunburn will probably need medical treatment.

You can revise the sentence by changing *with the bad sunburn* to the verbal *badly sunburned* and placing it before *teenager:*

> The badly sunburned teenager in the pool will probably need medical treatment.

In the next example you find the adjective clause *who eats candy* modifying *person.* The second modifier—*with decayed teeth*—seems to modify *candy* instead of *person:*

> The person who eats candy with decayed teeth frequently suffers extreme pain.

The sentence probably has to be changed completely:

> The person with decayed teeth frequently suffers extreme pain when eating candy.

DANGLING MODIFIERS

A modifier "dangles" because it has no noun in the independent clause to modify. (*DM* is the correction symbol for *dangling modifier.*) Sometimes a dangling modifier results if you leave out words needed to explain something clearly. In the following example, the verbal phrase *Seeing the lights* does not explain who was seeing the lights, and the independent clause does not give this information either. Because of its position at the beginning of the sentence, the verbal phrase seems to modify *city:*

> *Not:* **Seeing the lights,** the city was beyond the small hill.

Actually the verbal should modify a noun such as *passengers:*

> *But:* **Seeing the lights,** the passengers in the bus knew that the city was beyond the small hill.

To rewrite a sentence with a dangling modifier, you can break it into separate sentences. You may have to supply additional information before you rewrite the sentence. In the following example *While watching television* seems to say that the doorbell was watching television. Revise the sentence by adding a subject that tells who was watching television:

> *Not:* **While watching television,** the doorbell rang.
> *But:* **While Lisa was watching television,** the doorbell rang.
> *Or:* **While watching television,** Lisa heard the doorbell ring.
> *Or:* Lisa was watching television when the doorbell rang.

If you change the order of the modifier and independent clause, you still have the same problem:

> *Not:* The doorbell rang **while watching television.**
> *But:* The doorbell rang while Lisa was watching television.
> *Or:* When the doorbell rang, Lisa was watching television.
> *Or:* When Lisa heard the doorbell ring, she was watching television.

Dangling modifiers may also result when the verb in the independent clause is passive (*be* + V-ed) and the doer is not included in the sentence:

> *Not:* **By selling the house,** the retirement account was increased.

Before rewriting the sentence, ask who was selling the house. The subject might be *the widow:*

> **By selling the house,** the widow increased the retirement account.

An infinitive verbal phrase can also become a dangling modifier when the verb in the independent clause is passive:

> *Not:* **To open the bank account,** five forms must be filled out.
> *But:* **To open the bank account,** the applicant must fill out five forms.

A verbal phrase may be a dangling modifier if the word it should modify is a possessive modifying the subject of a sentence. In the next sentence *Using a special paste wax* cannot modify *Jesse's,* a possessive that modifies *car.* The sentence has to be rewritten with *Jesse* as the subject:

> *Not:* **Using a special paste wax,** Jesse's car began to shine.
> *But:* **Using a special paste wax,** Jesse made his car shine.

EXERCISE 20D

Revise the following sentences to eliminate misplaced or dangling modifiers. If you cannot decide how to rewrite the sentence, write each idea in the sentence as separate simple sentences. Then combine the simple sentences.

EXAMPLE: Glancing at his watch, no time was lost in leaving for the airport.

~~Steve was~~ glancing at his watch.   Glancing at his watch, Steve lost
Steve lost no time in leaving for   no time in leaving for the air-
the airport.   port.

EXAMPLE: The boy gently stroked the soft, fluffy kitten, carrying a BB gun.

The boy gently stroked the soft,   The boy carrying a BB gun
fluffy kitten.   gently stroked the soft,
~~The boy was~~ carrying a BB gun.   fluffy kitten.

1. Lying in the sun, the beach was crowded with people the whole weekend.

2. The woman with the big hat from Chicago buys and sells valuable stamps.

3. Chopped in the grinder, the baker added nuts to the cake batter.

4. At the age of ten, Sandy's grandfather took her to Europe.

5. Looking out the windows of the Empire State Building, the New York skyscrapers
were seen by the tourists.

6. Falling to the floor, there was a loud crash of the vase.

7. It was decided by the driver to turn off the freeway, confused by the traffic signs.

8. While putting a new bulb in the ceiling fixture, the ladder slipped, and Karl fell to the floor.

9. After completing the physical examination, the examining room should be cleaned.

10. The man who carried bricks with blistered fingers got a bad infection in his hands.

11. Flying through the night sky, the stars were seen clearly from the plane.

ASSIGNMENT: Infinitive Phrases

Write a paragraph of about eight to ten sentences about communication. You might discuss some aspect of newspapers, television, radio, motion pictures, or computers. First, write your ideas down in a series of sentences. Then revise what you have written by connecting and combining sentences to show the relationship of ideas clearly. Use infinitive phrases and other verbal phrases wherever they are appropriate. Underline all the infinitive phrases in your paragraph. Label the paragraph *Infinitive Phrases,* and hand it in to your instructor.

Lesson 21

The Absolute Phrase

In the last three lessons, Lessons 18, 19, and 20, you have been combining sentences by deleting words and changing verbs in some sentences to verbals. You can combine the following set of sentences in similar fashion, but the phrases will be absolute phrases. An absolute phrase has a subject but only a part of the verb:

SENTENCES	ABSOLUTE PHRASES
The hundred-year-old man opened his birthday present.	— The hundred-year-old man opened his birthday present, **his hands trembling, his voice quavering with excitement.**
His hands ~~were~~ trembling.	
His voice ~~was~~ quavering with excitement.	

The absolute phrase contains an idea closely related to the idea in the independent clause. Because it is a phrase, it cannot stand alone as a sentence; it is a fragment, a part of a sentence. Therefore, it must be attached to an independent clause.

Before you look at more examples of absolute phrases, review verbal phrases in the following example. On the left is a set of single sentences; the subject of each sentence is the same—*girl* and *she.* On the right is the combined sentence with verbal phrases; *screamed* became *screaming,* and *caught* became *catching:*

SINGLE SENTENCES	COMBINED SENTENCE
The tall, slim girl rushed wildly through the woods.	The tall, slim girl rushed wildly through the woods, **screaming frantically** and **catching her waist-length hair on the bushes momentarily.**
~~She screamed~~ frantically.	
~~She caught~~ her waist-length hair momentarily on the bushes.	

The following example demonstrates how some sentences in a set can be changed to absolute phrases. Notice that the set of single sentences on the left is similar to the set in the example above; however, the subject of each of the sentences below is different—*girl, screams,* and *hair.* The absolute phrases in the sentence on the right retain the subjects *screams* and *hair,* and the verbs *echoed* and *was caught* become verbals—*echoing* and *catching:*

SINGLE SENTENCES	COMBINED SENTENCE
The tall, slim girl rushed wildly through the woods. Her screams echoed among the trees. Her waist-length hair was caught momentarily on the bushes.	The tall, slim girl rushed wildly through the woods, **her screams echoing among the trees, her waist-length hair catching momentarily on the bushes.**

If you write adverbial clauses showing time or cause, you can usually change them to absolute phrases. In the first three examples below the past perfect tense forms of the verb *had arrived, had sounded,* and *had failed* are changed to the perfect tense forms of the verbals—*having arrived, having sounded,* and *having failed:*

ADVERBIAL CLAUSE	ABSOLUTE PHRASE
After the luggage had arrived, the tourists dressed for dinner.	**The luggage having arrived,** the tourists dressed for dinner.
After the dinner gong had sounded, the guests took their places at the tables.	**The dinner gong having sounded,** the guests took their places at the tables.
Because the student had failed the test, the teacher gave him another form.	**The student having failed the test,** the teacher gave him another form.

In the next example *was* becomes *being* in the absolute phrase:

Lucas had to make all the decisions for the family **because Malcolm was in Scotland.**	Lucas had to make all the decisions for the family, **Malcolm being in Scotland.**

Sentences with a form of *be* as the verb can be changed to absolute phrases by deleting the verb:

SINGLE SENTENCES	COMBINED SENTENCE
The new renter struggled up the stairs. A heavy suitcase ~~was~~ in one hand. A bird cage ~~was~~ in the other.	The new renter struggled up the stairs, **a heavy suitcase in one hand, a bird cage in the other.**

Absolute phrases may appear at the beginning, in the middle, or at the end of a sentence. They are enclosed in commas to separate them from the rest of the sentence.

EXERCISE 21

Combine the following sets of sentences by making one an independent clause and the others absolute phrases. First, write X before the base sentence. Second, change the verb to a verbal in each sentence that is to become an absolute phrase. Finally, attach the absolute phrase to the independent clause, and write the combined sentence.

EXAMPLE: The furniture ~~had been delivered~~
             to the model home.   **Verbal: having been delivered**
         X   The interior decorator helped the delivery people place the pieces in
             the rooms.

             The furniture having been delivered to the model home, the interior
             decorator helped the delivery people place the pieces in the rooms.

1. X   The huge black dog growled viciously.
       His white teeth snapped menacingly.   **Verbal:**
       His body was positioned to attack.   **Verbal:**

2. X   Jody's face had been battered in the accident.
       His lips were swollen and bleeding.   **Omit verb:**
       His forehead was cut deeply.   **Omit verb:**

3.   The snowstorm delayed Jonathan's plane.
       The executive committee meeting was delayed for three hours.

4.   The ship floundered in the storm.
       Its sails were shredded by the wind.
       Its mast was broken in two.

5.   The couple had received the inheritance.
       They paid their debts.
       They bought a new car.
       They gave their children gifts.

6.   The house was a disaster after the tornado.
       The windows were cracked or broken.
       The doors were torn from their hinges.
       The whole frame was pushed slightly off the foundation.

7.   Russell had photographed all the damage.
     The insurance adjuster was able to include the pictures in his report.

ASSIGNMENT: Absolute Phrases

Write a paragraph that consists of eight to ten sentences when it is completed. You might write about social customs and folklore—origins of customs, the need for patterns of living, development of customs, and other similar topics. First, write your ideas down in a series of sentences. Then revise what you have written by connecting and combining sentences to show the relationship of ideas clearly. Try to include three or four absolute phrases in your paragraph. Underline the absolute phrases. Label the paragraph *Absolute Phrases,* and hand it in to your instructor.

Lesson 22

Revising and Editing

You have been able to observe the flexibility of language as you have written sentences and then connected and combined them to make your writing cohesive and to relate ideas logically. You may have found that some sentences you have written are slightly awkward, or the combined sentence may change the meaning of what you intended to say. These kinds of problems are not unusual for writers. Though you may take advantage of this flexibility to manipulate language and clarity meaning, you may not always exert the control you need to keep from writing confusing sentences. In your eagerness to make your writing more compact, you may delete more words than you should. Or you may place one idea in a relationship with another idea that changes the meaning of the sentence completely or makes no sense at all. In the following example the writer intended to make one statement, but she wrote another one instead:

> Then she got the notion of what fun it would be a princess lost in the forest and have a handsome prince save her from a beast or a heroic mountain climber, but her dreams were always like that.

The three main problems in the sentence above are omitting necessary words, misplacing words, and using the wrong connectors. The omitted words have been added in bold type in the example below. The misplaced words are *a heroic mountain climber.* The connector *but* at the beginning of the last sentence below causes confusion because the sentence following is not actually in contrast with the preceding ideas. The writer probably should have omitted *but* or used *happily* or *unfortunately,* depending on the meaning she intended. If you break the sentence into its essential parts, you can then see what the writer intended:

Then she got the notion of ~~something~~ **/** .
What fun it would be **to be** a princess lost in the forest.
/AND/ ~~What fun it would be~~ **to** have a handsome prince **/** save her from a beast.   **/;/**
/OR/ ~~What fun it would be~~ **to have** a heroic mountain climber ~~save her from a beast~~.
~~But~~ happily (unfortunately) her dreams were always like that.

The revised sentence then reads as follows:

> Then she got the notion of what fun it would be to be a princess lost in the forest and to have a handsome prince or a heroic mountain climber save her from a beast; happily her dreams were always like that.

Such revision is an important part of writing because it gives you a second, third—even a fourth or fifth—chance to change or clarify the presentation of your ideas. Now that you have studied ways to organize your ideas, to connect and combine sentences, and delete unnecessary words, you are well equipped to make revisions that will improve your paper.

Once you have completed the first draft, put it aside. In a day or two try reading it as if you had never seen it before. Does the paper make sense? Is it well organized? Do you find confusing passages? Mark these places so that you know what parts to look at again when you begin revising the paper.

The second time you read through the paper, note the length of the sentences. Some should be short and others long to give variety to your writing style. If you find several short sentences, read them carefully, and decide whether you can combine them. If, on the other hand, you discover a long, involved sentence that is difficult to understand, break it into two or three parts, using transitions where they are needed.

When you examine your paper the third time, read each sentence carefully. If it has grammatical errors or it needs punctuation, make the necessary changes. Check the spelling, and use a dictionary to find the words that might be misspelled.

After you have made all the changes, prepare the final copy according to the instructions your instructor has given you. Then hand it in.

When you give your paper to an instructor to evaluate, he or she acts as an editor, reading the paper and making suggestions for improving your presentation. These suggestions may be short notes written in the margins, grammatical terms that identify a problem, or correction symbols, a shorthand form that instructors use instead of writing out the complete label.

You may use the checklist on the inside back cover to review each of your papers before you copy the final draft or to interpret the notes your instructor/editor has made. The list contains references to lessons in which you can find detailed explanations of the terms and constructions, which you have already studied.

EXERCISE 22

The sentences in this exercise are awkward and confusing, sometimes because the relationship of ideas is not shown clearly and sometimes because of grammatical problems. As you read each sentence, try to understand what the writer means. You might break the sentence into separate sentences to examine what each part of the sentence is saying. Or you may have to add words to develop an idea that is not clearly or fully expressed. Write your revision in the space below the sentence.

EXAMPLE: The oil caught fire and was spread quickly through the building by high winds common to the region.

Your thinking might be something like the following: The first part of the sentence above is about oil catching fire. The second part, beginning with *and* says that something *was spread quickly through the building.* The way the sentence is written, the writer is saying that oil was spread, but it seems unlikely that wind would spread oil. The writer probably means that fire was spread:

The oil caught fire.

_____?_____ was spread quickly through the building by high winds common to the region.

Revision: The oil caught fire, and the fire was spread quickly through the building by high winds common to the region.

Or: The oil caught fire, and the high winds common to the region quickly spread the fire through the building.

1. We request that once you have received your bus ticket, you stay in the waiting room, relax, and have an enjoyable day in Juneau.

2. Mike looked at the sun breaking through the morning mist, surrounded by the clearest sky he had ever hoped to see.

3. Swooping birds and crawling bugs stirred about with an occasional hum from a nearby grove of trees.

4. Frozen in places, Harvey listened to the branches tear and snap as the wind beat them against the cabin.

5. Clara noticed a small bird whisking by again and again, and saw it making a nest. Upon longer study she saw there were two birds that worked together closely and it was this bond that made them seem like one, and created the nest before her eyes.

ASSIGNMENT: Revising and Editing

Write a paragraph about a topic that you really enjoy discussing. Before you copy the final draft to hand in, use the checklist on the inside back cover to review your paragraph. Then revise awkward sentences, and remove grammatical problems. Label the final draft *Revising and Editing,* and hand it in to your instructor.

Review

I. Connecting and Combining
   (40 points—5 points each sentence)   Score _____

Connect and combine the following sets of sentences. In some cases you will be able to combine the sentences by changing verbs to verbals. In other cases you will use ways to connect and combine sentences that you have studied in preceding lessons. First, read the sentences in the set. Second, place X before the sentence you choose for the base sentence. Third, cross out unnecessary words. Fourth, change the verbs to verbals wherever you can. Fifth, add connectors, or make any other appropriate changes. Finally, combine all the sentences in a set into a single sentence.

EXAMPLE: X   The "gates of hell" / revealed a source of energy / .
              ~~They were~~ discovered by a surveyor / .   **/, V-ed/**
              ~~The surveyor was~~ on a bear-hunting expedition / .
              ~~It was~~ in 1847.   **/,/**
              ~~The source of energy is~~ now harnessed to produce electricity for northern California.   **/V-ed/**

              The "gates of hell," **discovered by a surveyor on a bear-hunting expedition in 1847,** revealed a source of energy **now harnessed to produce electricity for northern California.**

1.   Explorers visited the mountain site later.   **/V-ing/**
        X   Explorers / discovered something / .
   /THAT/ The mysterious white plumes of steam came from / steam vents / .
              The steam vents were small.   **/,/**
              The steam vents were natural.
              The vents were in the earth's surface.

2.   X   In the late 1800s the area / became a tourist attraction / .
                 It was situated 1,700 feet above sea level.   **/, V-ed,/**
                 It was named *The Geysers.*   **/V-ed/**

3.   X   In the 1920s people thought something / .
/(THAT)/   They wanted to harness the underground steam.   **/,/**
   /BUT/   They could not find / suitable equipment / .
    /OR/   They could not develop suitable equipment.
                 The equipment was needed to do the job.   **/V-ed/**

4.   Drilling companies finally began working in the 1950s.
               In 1967 three drilling companies joined together.
               They presently supply a California electric company with steam for its generators.

5.   The electric company now operates the largest geothermal plant in the world.
               The electric company has fifteen units in operation.
               The units generate electricity.

6.   Steam comes from almost a mile beneath the earth's surface.
               Steam generates almost enough electricity to serve San Francisco.
               Steam from the fifteen units saves fossil fuels.
               Steam provides the equivalent of more than nine million barrels of oil a year.

7.   The steam rises through holes.
     The holes are drilled in the earth's surface.
     The steam produces tremendous pressure.
     The pressure hits turbine blades.
     The pressure spins the blades rapidly.
     The pressure drives the generator to produce electricity.

8.   More companies are drilling in the area for steam.
     Other utilities and public agencies will build electricity-generating
     plants.

II. Revising and Editing
(60 points—3 points each)   SCORE _____

The following paragraph contains twenty writing problems that should be eliminated.
They may be sentence errors, such as comma splice, run-on, or fragment; grammatical
errors, such as subject-verb agreement, pronoun-antecedent agreement, tense, or misplaced modifier; or stylistic problems, such as parallelism, overuse of passive verbs, or
the need for transitions. Read the entire paragraph so that you understand what it is
about. Then revise it to eliminate the problems. For correction symbols, see the checklist on the inside back cover.

SV Agr   *PA Agr*   *Frag*
    A teen-ager sometimes have trouble living with their parents. One solution to

run away from home. Another solution is made possible in Connecticut by a new

Run-on   *Trans*   *Pass*
law children can "divorce" their parents. A legal separation was wanted by David

         P   *SV Agr*   *Frag*   *P*
from his mother who have a drinking problem. And from his father who works in

                                                                    CS
Saudi Arabia for an oil company. David is now recognized by law as an adult, he can

*Paral*_____
sign legal contracts, getting married, joining the military, and establishing residency.

Trans   *Trans*
Parents can "divorce" their unmanageable children sixteen or older. Laura's parents

wanted her to go to college. *Tense* They give her a car, clothes, and money. Laura is

P *HM* _____
rebellious drinking heavily, staying out all night, taking drugs. Before moving to

___ *Pass* *Tense*
Florida, a legal separation was asked for by her parents. Laura is as relieved as they

were.

Answer Key

EXERCISE 1C

a. 1 Sports
    2 Baseball
    2 Tennis
    2 Golf
    2 Football
    2 Soccer
    2 Swimming

b. 1 Modes of transportation
    2 Fuel-powered vehicles
      3 Automobile
      3 Truck
      3 Motorcycle
    2 People-powered vehicles
      3 Bicycle
      3 Tricycle
    2 Horse-drawn vehicles
      3 Wagon
      3 Carriage
      3 Buggy
      3 Chariot

c. 1 Liquids
    2 Fuel
      3 Gasoline
      3 Alcohol
    2 Drinks
      3 Water
      3 Tea
        4 Herbal tea
      3 Coffee
        4 Decaffeinated coffee
    2 Alcoholic drinks
      3 Liquor
      3 Wine
      3 Beer

1 United States
  2 States
    3 Georgia
      4 Atlanta
    3 Illinois
      4 Chicago
    3 Texas
      4 Dallas
      4 Houston
    3 California
      4 San Francisco
      4 Los Angeles
      4 San Diego

EXERCISE 2C

1. b, f, k   2. a, j, n   3. e, g, m, r
4. i, l, o, q   5. c, d, h, p

EXERCISE 3A

Adjectives
1. Forty-three, noisy, the, small, kinder-garten
2. Those, large, white, a, blue, velvet, matching
3. The, nervous, their, American, valuable
4. Tom's, his, eighty-year-old, the, college, graduation
5. The, San Francisco, the, unknown, artists'
6. This, season's, popular, an, old-fashioned

Note: Answers for the sentence-combining exercises are suggested. Check with your instructor if you have written a sentence differently.

EXERCISE 3C

Sometimes <u>overweight</u> people decide to lose <u>excess</u> pounds by cutting calories. <u>Their</u> <u>new</u> diets may consist of <u>eye-appealing</u>, <u>taste-tempting</u> <u>fruit</u> or <u>vegetable</u> salads. However, <u>the</u> <u>unsuspecting</u> dieters may not be aware that <u>some</u> <u>salad</u> ingredients are <u>high-calorie</u> foods even in <u>small</u> amounts. For example, <u>kidney</u> or <u>garbanzo</u> beans and <u>macaroni</u>, <u>potato</u>, and <u>bean</u> salads contain about <u>120–180</u> calories in <u>each</u> <u>half</u> cup. Even <u>cottage</u> cheese contributes <u>120</u> calories in <u>a half</u> cup, but <u>the</u> calories are even <u>higher</u>—<u>225</u> calories—in <u>shredded</u> <u>cheddar</u> or <u>Swiss</u> cheese. <u>The</u> <u>worst</u> offenders are <u>the</u> <u>delicious</u>, <u>mouthwatering</u> salad dressings—from <u>240</u> to <u>300</u> calories in <u>a</u> <u>three-tablespoon</u> scoop. Dieters can choose instead <u>filling</u>, <u>low-calorie</u> vegetables. <u>The</u> list includes lettuce, <u>shredded</u> cabbage, <u>regular-size</u> or <u>cherry</u> tomatoes, <u>sliced</u> cucumbers, <u>cauliflower</u> buds, <u>sliced</u> mushrooms, <u>carrot</u> slices, and <u>green</u> <u>pepper</u> strips. <u>A</u> <u>lemon</u> or <u>buttermilk</u> dressing can also eliminate <u>unwanted</u> calories.

EXERCISE 3D

1. The short, bald manager asked the noisy crowd to listen to him.
2. The nervous, perspiring manager made a brief announcement.
3. The small company could not give the employees medical and dental benefits.
4. Three angry employees demanded an immediate explanation.
5. The red-faced manager begged the agitated employees to listen again.
6. He explained that the president of the company had authorized an immediate 10 percent raise.
7. The excited, happy employees quickly spread the good news about the raise.

EXERCISE 3E

1. Carefully (how), regularly (when), recently (when), once a week (when)
2. Once a month (when), out (where), systematically (how)
3. Soon (when), brightly (how), profusely (how), everywhere (where)
4. badly (how), once a week (when)
5. Eventually (when)
6. pleasantly (how), sweetly (how)

EXERCISE 3G

1. The experienced, enthusiastic manager spoke encouragingly to six eager salespeople.
2. The five bright red telephones rang almost constantly the whole day.
3. Curious customers came into the newly decorated office and sat in the comfortable chairs for an hour or more.
4. At the end of the day the happy, successful salespeople reviewed the two sales and prospects for ten sales.

EXERCISE 3H

1. The second hour *or* Next
2. The third hour *or* Then
3. At noon *or* After that
4. In the afternoon *or* After lunch

EXERCISE 4A

. . . in their yards. They eat . . . they want, and then they preserve . . . in the winter. They find cleaning . . . consuming. They then . . . . Next, they store . . . .

EXERCISE 4E

1. Maria and Paul are expert cooks, and they create . . . their restaurant . . . .

2. Friends who dine with <u>them</u> receive
   . . . when ~~he~~ <u>Paul</u> brings . . . .
3. Another of <u>his</u> specialties is preparing . . . .
4. ~~She~~ <u>Maria</u> specializes in preparing . . . .
5. Each of the meals is served on ~~their~~
   <u>its</u> own special platter.
6. Maria's music group holds ~~their~~ <u>its</u>
   monthly meetings . . . .
7. . . . each member of the group orders ~~their~~ <u>his or her</u> favorite meal.
8. ~~Both~~ <u>Both</u> <u>Paul</u> and <u>Maria</u> take
   courses . . . .
9. They test the recipes . . . before preparing ~~it~~ <u>them</u> in the restaurant.
10. ~~One~~ <u>People</u> can learn to be ~~a~~ gour-
    met <u>cooks</u> if ~~one~~ <u>they</u> ~~has~~ <u>have</u> the
    time and the desire, but ~~one~~ <u>they</u>
    usually ~~has~~ <u>have</u> other interests
    competing for ~~one's~~ <u>their</u> time.

EXERCISE 5B

Verbs
1. confuse   2. disappear
3. examine

EXERCISE 5C

Portable kerosene heaters ~~pose~~ a
(posed / will pose)
threat . . . heaters ~~are~~ not vented. . . . car-
(were / will not be)
bon monoxide ~~fills~~ a room. The silent
(filled / will fill)
killer easily ~~overcomes~~ . . . heaters
(overcame / will overcome)
~~are~~ also a fire hazard. . . . the flame fre-
(were / will also be)
quently ~~ignite~~ . . . . A third danger ~~is~~ to
(ignited / was)
(will ignite) (will be)

Portable kerosene heaters ~~pose~~ a
    posed
    will pose
threat . . . heaters ~~are~~ not vented. . . . car-
    were
    will not be
bon monoxide ~~fills~~ a room. The silent
    filled
    will fill
killer easily ~~overcomes~~ . . . heaters
    overcame
    will overcome
~~are~~ also a fire hazard. . . . the flame fre-
    were
    will also be
quently ~~ignite~~ . . . . A third danger ~~is~~ to
    ignited   was
    will ignite   will be

small children who ~~touch~~ or ~~fall~~ on
    touched   fell
    will touch   will fall
the heaters. The hot metal ~~burns~~ them
    burned
    will burn
badly. . . . heaters ~~are~~ not safe . . . .
    were
    will not be

EXERCISE 5E

1. planned   2. had applied   3. had
saved   4. arrived   5. said
6. misses   7. has   8. enjoys
9. will become   10. will have saved

EXERCISE 5F

1. are working *or* were working
2. have been studying *or* had been
   studying
3. will be flying
4. is running *or* was running
5. will have been playing
6. has been riding *or* had been riding
7. will be taping

EXERCISE 5G

	AUXILIARY VERB(S)	MAIN VERB
1.	did	appreciate
2.		spent
3.	have been	seeing
4.	are	taking
5.	have	recommended
6.	should	exercise
7.	may	include
8.		meet, discuss
9.	are going to	stage

EXERCISE 5H

	SUBJECT	VERB
1.	Each	has

	SUBJECT	VERB
2.	You and Tina	are
3.	Reed (or) Grover	is coming
4.	group	intends
5.	None	like *or* likes
6.	Shari and Elaine	conduct
7.	(Neither) Brad (nor) brother	has
8.	supervisor	attends
9.	*The Warriors*	is
10.	team	go
11.	One	has appeared
12.	(Either) Sylvia (or) sister	owns
13.	Five dollars	seems
14.	Mathematics	presents
15.	suitcases	are
16.	dog	makes
17.	tent, fishing poles, and bait	are
18.	Everybody	wants
19.	floors	need
20.	Any	is *or* are

EXERCISE 5I

1. gather   2. have attended
3. had traveled   4. had discussed
5. chose   6. is   7. sit
8. bring   9. buy   10. will play   11. will provide   12. expects

EXERCISE 6A

1. A   2. A   3. X   4. A
5. X   6. X   7. A   8. A
9. X   10. X

EXERCISE 6B

(You may use connectors besides the ones indicated.)
1. . . . years later. She <u>also</u> examined. . . .
2. . . . left door. <u>In addition</u>, a long, narrow dent . . . .

3. X
4. . . . radiator hose. <u>Furthermore</u>, the brakes seemed . . . .
5. X
6. X
7. . . . one summer. She <u>also</u> made weekly trips . . . .
8. . . . a used car. <u>In addition</u>, she looked . . . .
9. X
10. X

EXERCISE 6C

(You may use connectors besides the ones indicated.)
1. . . . to Philadelphia, <u>AND</u> he put . . . .
2. . . . office to another; <u>moreover</u>, it offers . . . .
3. . . . in cargo planes; they can <u>also</u> be transported . . . .
4. . . . courses; in some areas they can <u>also</u> earn . . . .
5. . . . rental contract; <u>in addition</u>, he insisted . . . .
6. . . . paperback books; <u>besides</u>, it featured . . . .
7. . . . women's magazine; <u>futhermore</u>, she sold . . . .
8. . . . sales catalog; Joan <u>also</u> decided . . . .

EXERCISE 6E

1. . . . in the assembling of products; they load . . . transport them; <u>in addition</u>, they are involved . . . .
2. . . . the welding; the robots <u>also</u> paint cars.
3. . . . finishing wood; at a plant . . . cartridges; <u>AND</u> a motor assembly . . . .
4. . . . with the chemicals; robots, <u>moreover</u>, are able to save . . . .
5. . . . in the ocean, for example; robots can, <u>in addition</u>, work . . . people can; they are <u>also</u> better able . . . .
6. . . . as a human arm; <u>besides</u>, they can . . . screws; often they take . . . .

EXERCISE 6F

. . . everyone's budget; one shop, for example, sells . . . dollars; another sells them . . . dollars. In addition, the new mall . . . restaurants; two department stores in the mall also each have a restaurant. The artist needing supplies, moreover, can find . . . shops; AND musicians can find . . . another shop. Shoppers will want to spend several hours in the mall shops.

EXERCISE 7A

1. Stephanie hired new salespeople for the garden shop.
2. First, she organized a training program for the salespeople for the next week.
3. Next, she asked the manager in the garden shop to conduct the training program.
4. Finally, she prepared practice exercises for operating the cash register.

EXERCISE 7C

1. AS their heartbeat increases, they get a stomachache or a headache, AND they cannot focus their eyes.	Time Addition
2. . . . cope with stress BEFORE they are faced with an exam.	Time
3. . . . is reduced AFTER they attend the workshop.	Time
4. . . . beneficial WHEN it does not prevent	Time
5. WHEN students become too relaxed, they do not care	Time
6. . . . several steps AFTER they receive the exam.	Time
7. First, they should read the directions twice; second, they	Time Time
should underline . . . directions; third, they should review	Time

EXERCISE 8A

		Cause/ Reason
1c.	The security guard cleaned his gun carefully BECAUSE he wanted to be ready at all times.	b
2c.	SINCE Sandra likes to eat strawberries, she has planted	a
3c.	The car stopped suddenly BECAUSE a small dog chased	b
3d.	The car stopped suddenly WHEN a small dog chased	
4c.	BECAUSE Harley had fertilized the orange trees carefully, they produced	a
4d.	AFTER Harley had fertilized the orange trees carefully, they	
5c.	Maria's new car rusted . . . Minneapolis BECAUSE snow removal crews	b
5d.	Maria's new car rusted . . . Minneapolis AFTER snow	

EXERCISE 8C

1.	The security guard wanted to be ready at all times; as a result, he cleaned his gun carefully.	Cause Result
2.	Sandra likes to eat strawberries; consequently, she has planted fifty	Cause Result

3. A small dog chased a black cat across the road; therefore, the car stopped suddenly.　　　　Cause / Result

4. Harley had fertilized the orange trees carefully; hence they produced more oranges than usual . . . .　　Cause / Result

5. Snow removal crews had used salt on the roads, AND Maria's new car therefore rusted quickly the first winter . . . .　　Cause / Result

EXERCISE 8F

1. Oil is needed . . . engine BECAUSE it reduces . . . .　　Cause/reason

2. The oil must be . . . intervals SO THAT engine wear . . . .　　Purpose

3. Old oil is loaded . . . abrasives; as a result, an oil . . . .　　Result
   or BECAUSE old oil is loaded . . . abrasives, an oil . . . .　　Cause/reason

4. How often to change . . . answer BECAUSE so much . . . .　　Cause/reason

5. Oil sludge is most likely . . . speed BECAUSE the engine does not become . . . .　　Cause/reason

6. A delivery car . . . speed; consequently, the oil . . . .　　Result
   or SINCE a delivery car . . . speed, the oil . . . .　　Cause/Reason

7. Many companies . . . days SO THAT the operating life . . . .　　Purpose

8. BECAUSE synthetic oils . . . friction, they increase . . . .　　Cause/reason
   or Synthetic oils . . . friction; therefore, they . . . .　　Result

EXERCISE 9A

1. Jeff collects . . . coins; similarly, his brother collects . . . .

2. People on the east side of the river are AS enthusiastic AS people on the west side of the river about the new marina . . . .

3. Katie needs AS much help with her math problems AS Victor needs with his.

4. The clothing manufacturing company is hiring AS many people AS the furniture factory. or The clothing manufacturing company is hiring fifty people; similarly, the furniture factory is hiring fifty people.

5. The Blue Streak Auto Club members followed the same route through the mountains AS the Gasohol Gang.

EXERCISE 9E

1. Steve had planned to work as an accountant, BUT (; however,) he is . . . .

2. The adventure movie promised . . . year; nevertheless, it is one . . . .

3. The tomatoes . . . now; instead they are . . . .

4. On the one hand, Sylvia enjoys most pets; on the other hand, she cannot . . . .

5. The Johnsons have . . . years; however, they never . . . .

EXERCISE 10A

1. ALTHOUGH many people think . . . tunnels, caves may actually . . . . or Many people think . . . tunnels, YET caves may actually . . . .

2. ALTHOUGH most exploring . . . walking, the memorable parts . . . . or Most exploring . . . walking; nevertheless, the memorable parts . . . .

3. EVEN THOUGH cave "squeezes" generally . . . length, many cave explorers . . . . or Generally cave "squeezes" . . . length, BUT many cave . . . .

4. ALTHOUGH people . . . successfully, confident, thin cavers . . . . *or* People of all . . . successfully; <u>however</u>, confident, thin cavers . . . .
5. ALTHOUGH people explored . . . for light seventy years ago, today a miner's electric . . . . *or* Seventy years ago . . . light, <u>BUT</u> today a miner's . . . .

EXERCISE 10C

1. D 2. C 3. D 4. B
5. A 6. A 7. B 8. C
9. D 10. A

EXERCISE 10E

1. People who are blind . . . easily IF the teacher . . . .
2. Blind players can judge . . . guitar PROVIDED THAT they learn . . . .
3. Blind students usually . . . students UNLESS the instruction . . . .
4. The blind guitarist . . . home IF the lesson is available . . . .

EXERCISE 10G

1. IF (PROVIDED THAT) 2. IF
3. WHEN 4. WHILE (AS)
5. <u>Then</u> 6. SO THAT 7. WHEN *or* IF 8. BEFORE 9. BECAUSE
10. IF 11. BECAUSE

EXERCISE 11A

1. Desert snakes . . . day, <u>OR</u> they seek shelter . . . .
2. Snakes cannot . . . cold, <u>AND</u> they cannot . . . . *or* Snakes cannot . . . cold, <u>NOR</u> can they live . . . .
3. Some snakes . . . ground, <u>AND</u> others live . . . .
4. Snakes have no ears, <u>AND</u> they do not have movable eyelids. *or* Snakes have no ears, <u>NOR</u> do they have movable eyelids.

5. The jaws of snakes are loosely jointed, <u>AND</u> they are extremely flexible.

EXERCISE 11C

1. Either Jack arranges . . . today, or I . . . .
2. The superintendent wanted neither the increased staff nor the additional budget. *or* Neither did the superintendent want the increased staff, nor would he accept the additional budget.
3. The new officers will move the main office either to Chicago or Atlanta.
4. The old dishwasher needs both a new pump and a silverware basket.
5. Either the people must mail the tax returns by midnight, or they must pay a fine. *or* The people must either mail the tax returns by midnight or pay a fine.

EXERCISE 11D

1. Jake is both a karate expert and an excellent wrestler. *or* Jake is not only a karate expert but also an excellent wrestler.
2. Neither the principal nor the teachers want to attend the convention.
3. Either George will repair the tractor and plow the field, or he will hire Tom to do the plowing. *or* George will either repair the tractor and plow the field or hire Tom to do the plowing.
4. Judy will neither give Ben a job nor lend him any money.
5. The new senator has neither kept his campaign promises nor introduced legislation to meet his constituents' needs.
6. Not only has Celia exhibited her strength of character during the recent crisis, but she also has been a source of encouragement for many of her co-workers.

EXERCISE 12A

1. The Harringtons neglect their children; <u>indeed</u>, the children . . . .
2. Since the accident Jim Stone seems . . . world; <u>in fact</u>, he no longer . . . .
3. Senator Miriam Glass has . . . beginning; she has <u>actually</u> made . . . .
4. Joe Feldon was badly hurt . . . week; <u>obviously</u> he will . . . .
5. The church members frequently . . . causes; they will <u>surely</u> want . . . .

EXERCISE 12D

1. First, 2. Either 3. or
4. Second, (Next,) 5. Third, (Then)
6. Actually (As a result,) 7. Fourth, (Later) 8. obviously (certainly)
9. Indeed, (To be sure,) 10. finally, (therefore,)

EXERCISE 13

1. Dick Sanders planned . . . Thursday BECAUSE (IF) he had . . . .
2. He was prepared for the test, <u>BUT</u> (; <u>however</u>,) he was not prepared . . . . *or* ALTHOUGH he was prepared for the test, he was not prepared . . . .
3. AS (WHEN) he left his driveway, he noticed . . . minutes; <u>BUT</u> (; <u>however</u>,) AFTER he had turned . . . thoroughfare, he heard nothing more.
4. At the Department . . . easily; <u>then</u> (<u>next</u>,) he and . . . car, <u>AND</u> Dick headed . . . .
5. AS Dick approached the exit, another driver turned . . . exit; the other driver cut in front of Dick's car.
6. Dick slammed on the brakes immediately, <u>AND</u> (, <u>BUT</u> *or* ; <u>however</u>,) his bumper scraped . . . . *or* ALTHOUGH Dick slammed on the brakes immediately, his bumper . . . .

7. (<u>However</u>,) The other driver did not stop; <u>instead</u> he raced across the parking lot, <u>AND</u> he parked . . . .
8. AS the examiner shook his head in disbelief, he told Dick . . . .
9. BECAUSE Dick was still upset, he waited to make a left turn.
10. AFTER the examiner repeated his instructions, Dick turned right; <u>then</u> he headed . . . .
11. AS he approached the intersection, he put on his brakes; <u>BUT</u> (<u>nevertheless</u>,) the car . . . .
12. <u>First</u>, he grabbed the emergency brake, <u>BUT</u> the car kept moving; <u>then</u> he turned the wheels . . . .
13. Both he and the examiner were jolted AS the car jumped the curb <u>AND</u> smashed into a fire hydrant.
14. WHILE the examiner held . . . groaned, the fire hydrant snapped off; <u>then</u> a large column of water . . . .
15. AFTER people helped Dick . . . car, the left tire burst; <u>then</u> the car tilted left on its wheel rim.
16. WHILE Dick stood . . . head, the examiner put . . . shoulders; he suggested trying . . . .

EXERCISE 14A

1. The woman whose house had been burglarized called the police.
2. . . . the novel that concentrates on the author's . . . .
3. . . . peculiar to refugees who come to . . . .
4. Karen hired artists' models whom she used . . . .
5. . . . lived in castles that were destroyed . . . .
6. . . . man-made lakes that serve as . . . .

EXERCISE 14B

1. . . . the cruise ship that sailed through . . . .

2. The rooster that crowed every morning woke the neighbors.
3. In early spring birds that had migrated north landed in . . . .
4. The children built a treehouse that had three rooms.
5. The sailors who were on duty painted the hull . . . .
6. The young man who had bought a new car wrecked it . . . .

EXERCISE 14C

1. Mitzi works for a considerate employer who provides . . . .
2. Mitzi earns extra money that covers . . . .
3. . . . generous bonus that she uses for travel . . . .
4. . . . vegetable garden, which she takes care of . . . .
5. Mitzi sells most of the vegetables (that) she raises.
6. The extra income enables her to enjoy luxuries (that) she could not afford otherwise.
7. Her husband, who spends long hours traveling and seeing customers, seldom helps her with the garden.
8. Mitzi's eight- and ten-year-old daughters, who seem to enjoy the garden, help their mother. *or* Mitzi's eight- and ten-year-old daughters, who help their mother, seem to enjoy the garden.

EXERCISE 14D

1. . . . San Francisco for a week. His plan (decision) pleases Scott.
2. The promotion, which she had earned, came after many years. *or* The promotion that she had earned came after many years.
3. Marsha disliked everybody. Nelson could not stand her attitude.
4. Last week Candy lost the suitcase that she had packed with dirty clothes.

5. . . . Carlos had expected. The high cost (exorbitant price) disappointed him.
6. The newspaper that contained depressing reports lay on the coffee table.

EXERCISE 14E

1. . . . seven-day trip that they took . . . .
2. . . . historical sites that they had read about . . . .
3. . . . the *Mayflower,* which had been built in England . . . .
4. As Karen and Steve stood on the deck of *Mayflower II,* they tried to imagine the experiences (that) the 102 Pilgrims had had sailing . . . .
5. . . . Coolidge's home after they had visited his birthplace . . . .
6. Once again Steve and Karen put their imaginations to work as they thought about the night that Vice-President Calvin Coolidge heard . . . .
7. . . . to Calvin Coolidge, who became the thirtieth president.

EXERCISE 15A

1. Hans decided when he would drive through France.
2. Sonia knows that she will want a larger house soon.
3. Why Ted refused the promotion is a mystery.
4. The scholarship committee knows who will receive the award.
5. The well-trained athlete asked whether he qualified for the basketball team.

EXERCISE 16A

1. The owner and the manager asked several construction . . . .
2. The job included tearing down a small, vacant brick building and removing two diseased elm trees.

3. The owner accepted the lowest bid, and the manager set a date for beginning construction. *or* After the owner accepted the lowest bid, the manager . . . .
4. The rumbling of the bulldozers and the banging of the bricks dropping in a dump truck gave the manager a throbbing headache for two days.
5. The noise of the building crews continued in the following weeks, but (; however,) the manager gradually paid less attention to it.
6. Soon the warehouse and garage were completed; then the manager moved a desk and file cabinets into the new office in the warehouse.
7. The person in charge of repairs moved equipment for repairing trucks and forklifts into the garage.
8. The new work areas improved plant efficiency; as a result, the owner and the manager were pleased. *or* Because the new work areas improved plant efficiency, the owner and . . . .

EXERCISE 16B

1. One instructor taught students to design, (to) make, and (to) sell jewelry.
2. Another instructor taught life drawing, conducted fashion seminars, and photographed students' art work.
3. "Tubs" Reilly made huge ceramic jars and bowls and slender vases.
4. People wondered whether he was called "Tubs" because he was a huge man or because he made huge jars and bowls.
5. Students had opportunities to exhibit their art work in the gallery at the institute and (to) sell their art work to commercial buyers and individuals.
6. Students, teachers, and guests attended the annual ball at the institute just before Christmas; they spent the evening dancing, and they ate the Christmas foods arranged on the long table.

7. All those attending wore costumes, masks, and jewelry from various periods in history.
8. At midnight the director of the institute asked judges to examine the costumes, select three winners, and award prizes.

EXERCISE 16C

1. One child is a girl, and the other is a boy.
2. The girl is four years old, and the boy is two (years old).
3. Christine and Jason like to play in the swimming pool.
4. Janet and Bruce have taken swimming lessons at a local swimming school.
5. Janet has studied water ballet, and Bruce has played water polo.
6. Janet and Bruce enjoy swimming in their pool at home.
7. Janet and Bruce want their children to learn to swim.
8. The parents can teach the children themselves, or they can take the children to a swimming school.
9. Bruce enrolls Jason and Christine in the swimming school.
10. Jason soon learns to float, and Christine quickly learns to swim.
11. Later Jason swims to the instructor in the deep end of the pool, but Christine hesitates to go into the deep end.
12. Bruce and Janet are pleased with the children's progress.

EXERCISE 17A

1. Women admired the Chamber of Commerce president, the handsomest man in town.
2. The bread contains six ingredients: freshly ground whole wheat flour, honey, oil, salt, water, and yeast.

3. The widow proudly showed visitors an old china bowl, a replica of one in the British Museum.
4. Jan worked hard for the third prize, an old map of China.
5. The apartment owner, a suspicious, stingy, old man, insisted that the old couple move out.
6. Police found evidence, a skeleton and a gold ring, in a shallow grave.
7. The lawyer Walt Bricker prepared the wills for his clients Jessie Young and Brad Franklin.

EXERCISE 17B

1. Candy wanted detailed reference material in her library, in other words, an encyclopedia.
2. Gardeners can plant two kinds of beans—bush beans and pole beans. *or* Gardeners can . . . beans, namely, bush beans and pole beans.
3. The new luggage—a garment bag, a cosmetic case, and a Pullman case on wheels—belonged to the college graduate.
4. Clarissa likes to visit museums to look at women's costumes from certain periods in history, for example, dresses with huge skirts from the 1860s, Victorian dresses of the 1880s, and dresses the flappers wore in the 1920s.
5. Paolo has a dream: he wants to return to Venice, his home.
6. The director has chosen the cast for the melodrama: (—) Donna Taylor, the heroine; Ward Cummings, the hero; and Dell King, the villain.
7. Some children face living with permanent handicaps, namely, (for example,) serious mental and physical disabilities. *or* Some children . . . handicaps—serious mental . . . .
8. On his ranch the farmer raised four grains: (—) wheat, rice, barley, and rye.

EXERCISE 17C

1. Stan, Debbie's brother-in-law, smokes two packs of cigarettes a day, drinks a six-pack of beer, and gambles every chance he gets.
2. Gordon, a dentist (,) who will have a vacation soon, plans to paint the house and prune the trees. *or* When Gordon, a dentist, has his vacation, he plans to paint the house and prune the trees.
3. Celia met her friends, former neighbors, at the airport and drove them to her home.
4. Tomatoes, the San Marzano variety, which produced an oval-shaped fruit, grew tall in the greenhouse. *or* Tomatoes, the San Marzano variety, grew tall . . . and produced . . . .

EXERCISE 17D

1. The experienced, knowledgeable buyer, a man of about forty-five, has the respect of the employees. *or* The buyer, an experienced, knowledgeable man of about forty-five, has . . . .
2. Sandra, an entertaining actor and folk singer, is witty and intelligent.
3. The people at the town meeting supported the mayor's proposal for increased police protection immediately and enthusiastically and placed the measure on the ballot.
4. Dave Asher, manager of the downtown car wash, acted responsibly and sympathetically and settled the claim quickly. *or* Dave Asher, manager of the downtown car wash, acted responsibly, sympathetically, and quickly when he settled the claim.

EXERCISE 18A

	VERB	V-ING VERBAL
1.	has been smoking	
2.	adds	smoking, irritating
3.	is saving	camping
4.	likes	saving
5.	is	Fishing
6.	was working	purchasing
7.	spends	working
8.	is disturbing	complaining

EXERCISE 18B

1. The traveler, finding no food in the cupboard, went . . . .
2. Carla dislikes setting . . . .
3. The children, trying to confuse the teacher, changed . . . .
4. Gene, holding his throbbing head and moaning softly, searched . . . .
5. Mary prefers cooking meat . . . .
6. Moving to Texas was a new . . . .
7. The door leading to a small room has been . . . .
8. The chairman of the committee, speaking loudly and banging the table, told . . . .

EXERCISE 18C

1. After falling from the tree, Cary . . . .
2. Before climbing a tree again, Cary . . . .
3. Cary had had other accidents that were the . . . .
4. Lydia read a novel while waiting for . . . .
5. After Rosalee left home, her mother immediately . . . .
6. After spending the sunny day . . . river, Karen and her friends . . . .
7. While helping a friend . . . apartment, Tom hurt . . . .

EXERCISE 18D

1. The pilot, flying a single-engine plane, enjoyed . . . .
2. (While) Looking out the window, the pilot saw . . . but no people . . . .
3. He began worrying and wondering (*or* and wondered) . . . .
4. Hearing the plane engine sputter slightly, he quickly looked at the gasoline gauge and saw . . . .
5. Feeling his heartbeat quicken, the pilot told himself not to panic because he knew . . . .
6. . . . column of smoke rising from the chimney . . . .
7. He saw a long path that looked like an airstrip in the snow directly ahead; he headed for it, hoping he had . . . .
8. After the plane engine stopped, the plane glided . . . .
9. Coming closer, he realized the path . . . an airstrip; people wearing snowshoes had . . . . *or* . . . not an airstrip but a path that people wearing snowshoes had made.
10. As the landing gear . . . snow, the nose . . . embankment, and the tail . . . .
11. Hanging upside down . . . cockpit, the pilot slowly . . . belt and finally managed . . . .
12. Hunters ran . . . building, pulled . . . plane, and helped . . . out; then they took . . . .
13. The next day . . . station; soon the pilot . . . home, wondering . . . .

EXERCISE 19A

1. The outside . . . was painted by Charles . . . .
2. The original color had been discovered by scraping . . . (by him).
3. A light tan color . . . trim was found (by him).

4. Matching paints were mixed by Mel . . . .
5. The details . . . were emphasized by the contrasting colors.

EXERCISE 19B

1. Melinda Robinson redecorated the interior . . . .
2. Melinda chose wallpapers and paints to . . . .
3. Melinda removed the old wallpaper with Charles' help.
4. Melinda's sister made the draperies . . . .
5. Charles and Melinda purchased the Victorian furniture . . . .

EXERCISE 19C

	VERB	V-ED VERBAL
1.	was frozen	hidden
2.	is frosted	
3.	had been beaten	captured
4.	was bruised	injured
5.	had been stolen	prized
6.	will be borrowed	
7.	had taken	forbidden
8.	was given	amazed

EXERCISE 19D

1. Glaciers seen . . . Alaska, began forming . . . ago because snow that . . . .
2. Instead it changed to grains of ice that gradually fused . . . .
3. . . . mountains like mammoth bulldozers for about 3,000 years.
4. Deep gorges formed, carved out . . . .
5. As the glaciers . . . land, they carried . . . .
6. The weight of the ice and abrasive action left ridges carved into . . . .
7. As the glacial ice gradually melted, it filled with water the gorges that the glaciers had carved.

8. Huge pieces of ice breaking away from the face of the glaciers crashed into the water, causing huge waves and filling the inlets . . . .

EXERCISE 20A

	VERB	INFINITIVE VERBAL
1.	asked	to complete
2.	intends	to go
3.	was	to avoid
4.	did allow	to play
5.	was built	to hide
6.	saw	(to) cut
7.	made	(to) cry
8.	held	to keep

EXERCISE 20B

1. The family pretended to accept . . . .
2. The inspector hopes to convince . . . .
3. Virginia Carson told her publisher to spend . . . .
4. . . . wife ordered a very expensive ball gown to wear . . . .
5. . . . find another speaker to replace . . . .

EXERCISE 20C

1. . . . terminal to catch the plane.
2. Richard to make . . . .
3. . . . shocked to receive . . . .
4. Otto expected to travel . . . immediately to open . . . .
5. . . . caused him to lose his job, his wife, and his best friend.
6. Because the plant manager wanted to explain . . . policy and to get support . . . state, he (she) spoke . . . .

EXERCISE 20D

1. People lying in the sun crowded the beach . . . . *or* The beach was crowded with people lying in the sun . . . .

2. The Chicago woman with the big hat . . . . *or* The woman with the big hat who comes from Chicago . . . .
3. The baker added nuts, chopped in the grinder, to the cake batter. *or* To the cake batter the baker added . . . .
4. Sandy's grandfather took her to Europe when she was ten. *or* . . . took her at the age of ten . . . .
5. Looking . . . Building, tourists saw . . . .
6. There was a loud crash as the vase fell to the floor.
7. The driver, confused by the traffic signs, decided . . . .
8. While putting . . . fixture, Karl fell to the floor when the ladder slipped. *or* While Karl was putting . . . .
9. After the doctor completes the physical examination, the nurse (the aide) should clean the examining room.
10. The man with blistered fingers who carried bricks got a bad . . . . *or* The man with blistered fingers got a bad infection in his hands when he carried bricks.
11. Flying . . . sky, passengers (the pilot) saw stars clearly . . . .

EXERCISE 21

1. The huge black dog growled viciously, his teeth snapping menacingly, his body positioned to attack.
2. Jody's face . . . accident, his lips swollen and bleeding, his forehead cut deeply.
3. The snowstorm having delayed Jonathan's plane, the executive committee meeting was delayed . . . .
4. . . . in the storm, its sails shredded by the wind, its mast broken in two.
5. The couple having received the inheritance, they paid . . . , bought . . . , and gave . . . .

6. . . . after the tornado, its windows cracked or broken, its doors torn from their hinges, and its whole frame pushed slightly . . . .
7. Russell having photographed all the damage, the insurance adjuster was able . . . .

EXERCISE 22

1. We . . . ticket, you stay in the waiting room and relax. We hope you have an enjoyable day in Juneau.
2. Mike looked at the sun, surrounded by the clearest sky he had ever seen, break through the morning mist. *or* Mike, surrounded by . . . .
3. Swooping birds flew about, and crawling bugs stirred. One (People in the area) could hear an occasional hum . . . .
4. Harvey listened to the branches, frozen in places, tear and snap . . . .
5. Clara noticed a small bird whisking by again and again and saw it making a nest. Later she realized two birds were working so closely together that they seemed to be just one bird building the nest.

Index

TO THE STUDENT

You, the student, are the final test of the success of our textbooks. We need your reactions and ideas if we are to serve you better. Following is a simple questionnaire which, if you would take a few moments to fill it out, will greatly help us to publish more informative and interesting books for you and your instructor.

When completed, simply tear out the page, fold and staple it with the post-paid label showing, and drop it in the mail. Thank you.

Your Name (If you wish): _____ Date: _____

School: _____

Size of Class: _____

Your Major: _____

1. What did you like best about this book?

_____
_____

2. What did you like least about this book?

_____
_____

3. Which chapters were easiest for you? Why?

_____
_____

4. Which chapters were most difficult for you? Why?

_____
_____

5. In general, how might the book be improved?

_____
_____

May we quote you in our advertising efforts?   Yes _____ No _____

Thank you,

Scott, Foresman, College Division
1900 East Lake Avenue
Glenview, Illinois 60025

Connecting and Combining (15317)
1 2 3 4 5 6 7

BUSINESS REPLY M